HOW TO BE

—

SUCCESSFUL

—

IN SPITE OF

—

YOURSELF

—

Ann Kaplan

HOW TO BE SUCCESSFUL IN SPITE OF ~~HIM~~ *YOURSELF*

PAGE TWO
BOOKS

Cataloguing in publication information is available from Library and Archives Canada.

ISBN 978-1-98902-540-6 (paperback)
ISBN 978-1-98902-541-3 (ebook)

Page Two Books
www.pagetwobooks.com
Cover design by Aldo Buzzolini
Cover photo by Kayla Rocca
Interior design by Peter Cocking and Setareh Ashrafologhalai
Interior illustrations by Ann Kaplan and Mark Hill
Editing by Carley Sparks

Printed and bound in Canada by Friesens

19 20 21 22 23 5 4 3 2 1

Distributed in Canada by Raincoast Books
Distributed in the US and internationally by Publishers Group West, a division of Ingram

annkaplan.com
@annkaplan_ownit

This book is dedicated to my first husband who
helped me realize that life is short, who showed me
I can make it as a single mother (without financial
support), and who inadvertently taught me that
I am the sole creator of my happiness.

*Personal note to my Ex: By the way, when you
outbid me at the art auction (yes, I saw that it was
you), I never wanted that painting. I was just
trying to donate to the charity—enjoy!*

CONTENTS

PROLOGUE

Dear Diary,

Remember I said I wanted a new project and if a publisher picked me up, I would write another book? Well, ta-da! I pitched one about my life, but they said the only thing trending right now are self-help books. So, I told them I had one of those in the making (and that I'd write a few things about my vagina). Anyway, I got a publisher! #hurray

Dear Diary,

It's been a week. Today, I decided to actually write the promised self-help book. And not just any book but one that is hysterically funny, one that does not depict (in any way) my own sad life, one that makes me appear to know all the secrets of the universe and to have been sent here on a mission to enlighten mere mortals on success! I AM GOD.

Dear Diary,

Okay, I have been avoiding you. It's just that my life seems to be on the verge of falling apart. I question if my marriage is good ... if I even believe in that institution (I don't). I'm struggling with the kids. And I'm beginning to think I might need a neck-lift! (I could always write the book during recovery ...) All of which leads me to believe that I may not actually be *qualified* to write a self-help book. But who is? I mean, seriously??

Dear Diary,

Progress! Sort of. I've combed through every self-help book I could get my hands on. (Try making *that* Indigo run without looking like a lunatic!) I considered googling "self-help" too, but I was worried that the Russians might find me. Turns out a lot of the people who write self-help books are, well, *just people*. Deepak Chopra used to smoke—he wasn't perfect! I think I might be qualified, after all ...

Dear Diary,

Pep talk. Since I last wrote, I've had my eyebrows tattooed (hence the jar of Vaseline on my bedside table), topped up on Botox, coloured my roots, and vacuumed. (Actually, the housekeeper vacuumed.) I have been *very* busy—just not busy writing the book. I'll start tomorrow!

Dear Diary,

False start. Today, I begin! I'm turning off my phone and my email. (Well, maybe just my email.)

Dear Diary,

STOP JUDGING ME.
  [*One year later...*]

Dear Diary,

You're not going to believe this, but... I've done it! I've *actually* written the book—and there's nary a vagina in it! (Let's hope no one notices.) It might even be good. Now, let's hope people read it... (Ack! What if no one buys it?!)

INTRODUCTION

I F YOU PICKED up this book, chances are you feel like you need a reboot, like something has to change and you want to invite more success into your life. You picked up a how-to because you *want to*. But if you're anything like me, there may be a story (or ten) in your past that still strikes a chord, a painful moment (or ten) that continues to resonate in your life and puts an *end to* your efforts.

For me, it started with a nose.

When I was young, I was told I was deformed. Not just slightly, but that my flat nose and odd features were the cause of great embarrassment for my family. "Ann was born without a nose," my adopted white parents would tell guests. "They can fix it when she's of age."

Not surprisingly, I spent a good deal of my childhood dreaming about the day I'd get a new nose. While other kids were thinking about buying new flare-bottomed Levi's, I was crossing out the years, then months, then days on my calendar until I could plant myself in front of a plastic surgeon to correct my God-given curse. *One day I'll be pretty . . .*

What I didn't know was that my nose was the result of an illicit tryst between my mother and an Asian entertainer. Rather than reveal the affair, she felt compelled to provide me with an explanation for why I looked different from my four sisters: I was not only adopted but deformed. I mean, who would question their mother?

For years, my parents struggled to live with that secret. I realized early on that I was a source of tension in their marriage, although I didn't understand why. I only knew that there was something wrong with me (physically) and that there was definitely something was wrong with how they communicated (*physically*).

Night after night, my mother would serve us a beautifully made dinner with homemade meringue for dessert, and my father would cap off the evening with a terrifying episode of domestic violence, punishment for her transgression. If only Mom had had the guts to pack up and go. She was so afraid to break up her family, so she took it for the team—again and again. If I could change anything in my past, it would be for her not to suffer for giving me life.

At age fourteen, I moved out. Scraggly, still underdeveloped (I could wear my bra backwards and it made no difference), and bearing the brutal knowledge that I was still four years away from getting a nose, I moved into a rented room in a house near school. I loved my parents dearly (in spite of all that crap), I missed my sisters desperately (I've never called them half-sisters), and I had to get a job. The hardest part was that no one in my family said, "Don't go." It was uneventful. I moved out, then I cried. (But no one knew.)

Fast-forward a few decades and, truth be told, I feel like I escaped somehow, slipped through the cracks. And I know I am far from being the only person to have a sad story to tell.

It's been years since I packed up my Clearasil and cotton undies. I have since found some balance in my life. I got a new nose, I found out the truth about my birth parents, and I somehow escaped the haunting memories of abuse. I've struggled through marriages (and failed), I've built businesses (and succeeded), I've written books, and I've been on television shows. Through it all, the most powerful lesson I've learned is how to live with joy in my heart, and that seems to be about as good as one can get.

It's from that place that I write.

When I started this project, I set out to write an advice book that showed my life, warts and all—the beatings, the infidelity, the horror of watching my family and dreams unravel, and my journey to try to find some element of happiness. I wanted to show that in spite of the crap you've been through, anyone can find hope—and even success.

As I started to write, crying over the abuse that I sugar-coated as "a learning experience," I was poignantly aware of the irony of wanting to change history—who I was and where I came from—whilst saying, "love who you are." I struggled with how much to share and feared that if I exposed the ugly parts of my past, I would be judged harshly. That by telling the truth, I would be seen as inadequate—a phony hiding behind Instagram posts that depict glamour and success. Then I worried that my life was too boring, that I was not interesting, and that no one would purchase the book, save for my ex-husband (and only to see if I gave him credit). One copy sold does not make a bestseller.

A million thoughts ran through my mind as I worked on the manuscript, but never once did I worry that I wasn't relatable enough—that is, until my publisher brought it up. Apparently, I'm too rich, too educated, too glamorous, too *reality star* to write a self-help book.

"So, if I appear as if I need help, if I am *not* successful, then I am relatable?" I replied. "For God's sake, I'll wear a garbage bag on the cover!"

Every woman knows you don't find success in life without digging through crap, and most want to change their life but don't realize they can. *It won't be about money*, I thought (but it is). *I've been married a few times, I'm self-made (well, parts of me are manufactured), I've got eight kids—and I'm happy!*

So I kept going, convinced that I had some wisdom to share. But I've learned in the process too. Originally, this book was called *How to Be Successful in Spite of Him*, a nod to the difficult lessons I've learned from the men in my past. I wasn't sure that would go over very well with my current husband, though, so I decided to change the last word to "yourself." (I could always change it back, I thought, depending on the state of our relationship closer to the book launch.)

But as I wrote the book, and as the #MeToo movement gained steam, I realized it was a moot point. One afternoon as I listened to *New York Times* reporter Jodi Kantor speak about the threats she received before breaking the Harvey Weinstein story, I was brought to tears and a new understanding.

"Were you afraid?" someone in the audience asked.

"I was afraid I would have all of this knowledge [of Weinstein's abuses], and the story wouldn't get out," she replied.

Little does she know, Jodi Kantor changed my life. I looked at these women—famous, successful women—who not only had the courage to come forward at significant risk to their careers and personal reputations, but who were survivors. In spite of what they'd been through, in spite of the men trying to hold them down, they went on to have successful careers, to have families, to thrive.

Like most women, I thought about my own experiences and I found power in the collective voice. I realized that it was never about "him." *He* is not going to get the reward for putting *us* beneath him in the first place. *He* is not taking blame or getting the accolades for where I am. *He* was never that powerful. The only person capable of creating my success or getting in its way is me. *I am successful because of me, not in spite of him.*

So . . . the title stayed *How to Be Successful in Spite of Yourself.*

The biggest elephants in the room are that marriage is a sentence, raising kids is tough, men can be abusive (and a lot of us hide it), and we all secretly want to be on a reality show. I was the right person to write this book because I've been through it and have managed to carve out some semblance of success. I think we all want to know how to have *that life*—the interesting job, the loving family, the supportive partner—but first we want to know how to get out of the crappy life we're in.

This is a book for those women who want out of mediocrity; the ones who look like they have "everything" but are hiding depression, sadness, or abuse; the ones who don't want to spend another day staring at a partner who long ago forgot how great they are (and they forgot too).

This book is for the ones who want more, the women who want it all.

And we can have it too.

(I)

THIS IS
SUCCESS

Upset that you're
a divorced, single mother?
Just imagine how you'd feel
if you were still married
to the jerk!

(1)

SUCCESS IS NOT A DESTINATION, IT'S A JOURNEY

---

*Success is liking yourself, liking what
you do, liking the way you do it.*

MAYA ANGELOU

N MY TWENTIES, my dream was to have ten children, work as an interior designer, and spend my days cooking, entertaining, and decorating the house while I looked after my perfect husband and our delightful family. By my thirties, I was well on my way to achieving that life. I earned a degree in interior design, I married a successful developer, and we had two beautiful boys. Then I discovered my husband had an avid interest in the waitress/real estate agent/accountant/girl at the corner store (see: all of the above). So that was the end of that.

I guess you could say he was perfect in a sense—*perfect he was gone.*

So there we were, the three of us (four if you count the cat). I realized that somehow I had to feed my children and be the chief cook and bottle washer, and that I would never have my dream house, let alone my dream.

Coming to terms with that loss, I felt profoundly alone, as though I had missed my chance at happiness. I'd wake up only to be tearful by the time I made it to the washroom. I cried at stoplights. I cried washing dishes. I cried whenever I found a moment to think about my pitiful existence. (Read: all the time.) At thirty-two, I was (somewhat) educated, still (relatively) young, and suddenly a single mother of two children (and a cat!) ... At least I was working. My only response in the face of this crisis was to cry.

The turning point came as I was leaning over the bathtub one evening, two little toddlers playing in a few inches of water. I was dutifully washing their hair when I started with the usual waterworks. My little boys looked up at me and, upon seeing my tears, burst into tears themselves. They were mirroring me. They were being what I was. In that moment, I came face to teary face with the hopeless message I was sending them. I decided then and there that, for them, I would get it together. I would take control of my life. I would follow my dreams and, what's more, I would do it with joy—it was just going to be a little harder (but "good" harder). If they were going to see me as a role model, then I owed it to them to be the best one I could be. Copy that, boys!

That was it. A hard line drawn in the sand. That was the first step on my path to success.

The New Normal

Everything in my life changed with the end of my marriage. I couldn't pay the bills and lost my home (my ex never paid the mortgage and, to this day, has never provided one dime of support). Suddenly the sole provider for my children, I had to cut back to a very tight budget. We moved from a house in the uppity Shaughnessy neighbourhood of Vancouver to a rental apartment so small I had to throw out my ex-husband's clothes to make room for the towels. I bought second-hand clothes and furniture, and I worked two jobs, subletting a room in my apartment in exchange for babysitting. I threw together an impromptu garage sale to pay for an emergency vet bill, and I once left a Rolex watch at the gas station as collateral while I scraped together twenty dollars to fill the tank (back in the day when twenty dollars could fill your tank!).

I made it work, and even though it was extraordinarily difficult at times, I never felt hopeless. I had next to nothing financially, but I had the ability to work. And so, when everything changed—and not for the better in a material sense—somehow I felt empowered. Walking away from that marriage was the hardest, and ultimately the best, decision I ever made. I realized that the only "thing" getting in the way of my success was *me*. Just because my life hadn't evolved in a way that matched my preconceived fantasy, just because the only thing that shined on my knight was his follically challenged

epidermal cap,[1] just because I was a single mom, didn't mean *that* would be my entire story.

Forget that! I rewrote the script. This wasn't going to be a sob story. It was going to be a success story—*my* success story.

It's funny how a change of perspective can change your life.

The Change That Changed Everything

My story isn't special or unique. Everyone experiences moments when it feels as if everything in their world has come crashing down around them—moments of profound loss or upheaval,

---

1   My editor suggested the word "scalp" here. (No one listens to their editor.)

losing a loved one or a job, a health scare. Those moments when life sends you reeling with a firm kick in the stomach. If you let them, those moments can offer a time for profound self-reflection. They force you to consider the path you're on, how you got there in the first place, and where you want to go. It's a time when we consciously and subconsciously seek change (or relief!). If we allow it, it can also be a time of renewal, when we implement the changes that will bring us happiness and, ultimately, "success."

For me, the end of my marriage was the spark that lit the fire. Going through that ordeal, I came to realize I had something I could use to achieve anything in life—a power that, when applied, could get me everything I wanted. In time, I found myself creating businesses, taking a small investment and turning it into millions. I used that power to attract desirable and interesting people into my life. And I harnessed the same power to assist me in raising a family and finding happiness—to take me from being a single mother of two toddlers in a rented apartment to living on an estate with multiple other properties at my disposal.

That power, that strength, that focus came from a realization that, in spite of where I came from, in spite of who I married (or who I left), in spite of the barriers in my way, the actions that I take today, this hour, this minute are the ones that will shape my destiny. That the power is in my own hands and in my own mind, and, conversely, that the limitations I put in my way are self-made as well. I realized that the only person responsible for who I am and how I live is me. And, what's more, I came to understand it was my own knowledge, accountability, and resolve that empower me to set the course for my future. *I* hold the power. And so can you.

What Is Success?

The first step to becoming "successful" is knowing what that term means to you. Some people define success as being rich, as having many children, as being happily married. I'm going to argue that it isn't necessarily any of those things. Success, I believe, is a state of mind. It's a feeling of completeness. Arguably, it's living your life the way you want to, intentionally and passionately, and being happy with who you are and where you are at every given moment. Success is something created from within.

Sure, with ignorance—oh, thank goodness for ignorance! it gets some people through very tough times—anyone can claim they feel they are living a life of success, while never seeking or understanding how they can do better. They can settle for the status quo, for what they feel they were born with or what they think they "deserve," all the while claiming, "Hey, I am happy where I am in life," never looking for a path that truly fulfills them.

But true success, in my mind, is a conscious way of living— one that embraces and aspires to your personal ideals. And what's more, it can be achieved by anyone! (Ignorant people aside.) You first have to know it is possible, then take the steps (the difficult steps) to make it happen.

If your goal is to be happy with who you are, then this is the right book for you.

Five Fundamental Truths about Success

Success can take many shapes. If you're an aspiring entrepreneur, maybe it's building your own business from the ground up. If you're climbing the corporate ladder, it could be the pro-verbial corner office. If you're a stay-at-home parent, your life's ambition could be to raise happy, healthy contributing members of society (this is achievable). Regardless of what you aspire to, there are certain truths about success that are universal.

1. Success Is a Choice

If you don't like something in your life and opt to not make change, that's your choice. But recognize that it *is* a decision. You've chosen to allow external forces to decide your destiny, and tomorrow you will be in the same place you are now because you *decided* to be there. You've chosen not to invite success into your life. If you picked up this book, though, chances are you don't fit this profile.

The opposite is also true. You can choose to strive for something different, something more. The power to change resides in all of us. It lies in the decisions we make today, and it is the power I have used to achieve everything I have in my life. I know that if I harness that power, if I use it now, then I can shape tomorrow and every day after it.

2. There Is No Expiry Date on Success

It is easy to feel, with each passing year, that starting from scratch is less and less feasible. We get to a point where we say, "It's too late" or "I am what I am"—or, my personal favourite, "Can't teach an old dog new tricks." Well, you can—at any age. But you must have the desire.

Whether you're in your twenties and trying to figure out your future career and your relationships (how does anyone ever make it through those difficult years?) or much older, more experienced, and more established, you have the opportunity right now, at this very point in time, to ask yourself, *What does success mean to me?* and *How can I be successful in the future?*

And then you can work to make those visions your reality. This is how Pulitzer Prize–winning author Frank McCourt achieved fame at age sixty-five after retiring from teaching. And why Dorothy Custer, the oldest living person in Twin Falls, Idaho, celebrated her 102nd birthday by BASE jumping off a 500-foot bridge above the Snake River. It's never too late or too early to pursue the life of your dreams.

3. Success Requires Effort

If you look at where you came from and where you are today, and feel frustrated or disappointed with your life, ask yourself: *Did I give up? Did I give it time? Did I put barriers in my own way?* More importantly, ask yourself: *If I had made different decisions, would I be in a better place now?* And if the answer is yes, ask yourself if you are willing to make the changes today to start building toward a better tomorrow.

Often, we make excuses for the state of our lives. We tell ourselves (and others) that we are comfortable where we are, that we are okay with mediocrity, or that we were not cut from the same cloth as high-achieving people. We rationalize our behaviours and lack of ambition by attributing them to something that has happened in the past. We blame our upbringing, a bad marriage, or a failed business. We may blame the loss of a loved one or bad habits we can't seem to shake. Whatever it is, we draw from our past as an excuse to not move forward, and then we let it weigh us down, like an anchor, keeping us exactly where we are. But we tell ourselves that it's okay, because the anchor is heavy.

Cutting ourselves free from the dead weight of our past requires sustained effort. The more you put in, the more you commit to letting it go and forging ahead with that which elevates and enhances your life, the greater the output will be. You will find yourself moving toward even greater success—more than you ever imagined.

4. Success Is a Way of Life

We've all experienced moments of success—times when you told a great story at a dinner table, or laughed with your friends over seeing eye to eye, or hit the ball out of the park in grade eight, or graduated with honours, or, or, or... Those *are* successful moments. But they alone do not make a life of success. You can fondly remember those moments, even reiterate them as MC at a wedding fifteen years later. And if they were great moments, hopefully you learned from them and know that you can have more of those moments—they were not your last.

Living a life of success, being regarded by others (if that's important to you) as successful, is not defined by a singular moment. (And please don't argue that you have had *two* moments—or even three! Those are still moments.) Success is a way of *being*. It is not an award (although you may collect them along the way) or a recognition. It's a way of life, a way of thinking.

Looking from outside, we would probably say that Mother Teresa led a life of success. Not because of the charity she founded or a particular child she helped, but by the way she lived her life—committed to the causes that moved her heart. Oprah Winfrey too has had many successes. We can argue over which one is her greatest, but the mere mention of her name conjures the image of a person who has been successful in her career, in giving of herself, and in life.

Success, in short, is a mindset. Even more importantly...

5. Success Can Be Learned

Successful people are sought after, they are the ones who are paid large dividends, asked to speak at conferences, and oft quoted in books such as this. The irony is that there is no barrier other than oneself to living a life of success.

Educators, philosophers, and leaders have long summarized the recipe for success, throwing out axioms such as "Think big, work hard, and persevere." All of those tenets are true. But the secret ingredient, the one that makes all the rest possible, is the simple realization that the only difference between you and the "oft quoted" is believing in yourself. If you believe you can be successful, if you take the steps to live a life of success, then you will *be* successful. It's as simple as that. Sometimes it's as simple as deciding you're no longer going to cry about your philandering ex-husband.

What If You Started Today?

My "aha" moment was triggered by the end of my first marriage, but you don't have to wait for your spouse to cheat on you or some externally imposed change in your circumstances. In fact, "waiting" itself is half the problem.

And we do it all the time. How often have you heard someone refer to their dreams in the past tense? "When I was younger, I wanted to be a dancer," people will say, or "I always wanted to have my own business." Then that statement is followed by a "but..."

"But I have a family to provide for now."

"But I have to look after my parents."

"But I didn't have the money to pay for school."

That *but* is the thing we hold accountable for where we are today. That *but* is the excuse that keeps us in the same place, the same situation, and the same state of mind—in perpetuity. We keep doing the same thing, downsizing our dreams and not creating new ones. We end up ten years from now, a decade older, living the same life and dragging our *but*s along with us.

But . . . what if we started right now and said, "Today will be different"? What if we looked at where we want to be tomorrow and where we want to end up in the future and decided that today we're setting new goals? What if we began to work toward achieving those new goals right this moment?

What if we took a step further? What if we looked at those goals—be it money or relationships or happiness—and said, "I want more"? What if we took away our perceived limitations and said, "I want it all!" and then decided we would take steps, immediately, to achieve it? Could we achieve it? Are we risking too much?

Therein lies our biggest challenge. The position we find ourselves in today is precisely the place where we are most comfortable. Even if we're not particularly happy in that place, even if we actively dislike where we're at in our career, relationships, health, or finances, it's familiar to us. It's what we know. Any new path, any divergence from the well-worn track we've been on, we think of as a "risk." But what if we amended that term and thought of every new path as an "opportunity"? When your older self looks back on you today, will that person be glad you made that change, or will you still be saying, "I should have done this or that"?

Success Starts with You

No matter who you are, whatever your age or economic background, if you have the dream and the drive, you can realize anything you set out to achieve. It is incredible what people can accomplish when they have hope. But the change, the shift in thinking, must first happen within you. The very first step is taking control of your headspace and knowing that you can start here and now, and that there's a way around every barrier in your path.

EXERCISE 1: Take the First Step Down Your Path to Success

If you want to make changes in your life and are willing to accept that, in order to be successful, you have to take a first step, you must mentally prepare yourself for the journey ahead. Start with this thought exercise:

1. **Be Open to Change:** Be open especially to change that lies outside your comfort zone. In order to find success in life, you will need to let go of old habits, consider new ideas and concepts, and possibly adopt a new way of life. You must be willing to make sacrifices and take on new challenges. If you want to be successful, you will need not only to be open to change but to embrace it.

2. **Be Mindful/In the Moment:** Pay attention to the moment. Commit yourself to understanding that your actions, in this moment, will affect you and the environment around you. To

be successful, you will take control, be present, and be aware—always—in the moment.

3. **Think Positive:** Change does not have to be a negative process. In fact, negative and critical behaviour can be destructive and crippling on your path to success. Negative thoughts will result in confrontation and defensiveness; they become fodder for petty gossip, discouragement, and/or distraction that ultimately leaves you with a bad feeling. Positive thoughts and actions, on the other hand, bring results. Positive thinking is not mired in excuses, nor is it necessarily sugar-coated half-truths. It is a choice to direct how we respond, and it is what enables a successful attitude. Same outcome, different action. To be successful, you will need to think and act as a successful person does.

4. **Practise Successful Behaviours:** People see their own success as something they have created. They may attribute some of it to those around them, but they generally do not see the whole picture—how their day-to-day interactions with others affect their successes. To truly find success, you need to learn from the casual exchanges you have with people (a coffee barista, 1-888 telemarketer...) and use those opportunities to practise expanding your network and drawing people in. You need to recognize those who will help you on your journey (and those who will not). To be successful, you must behave like a successful person; you must become associated with "success."

5. **Be Open to Winning:** Deciding to be successful means accepting that you will be different from your current norm. Your life will change, your thinking will change, and (especially

to those around you) *you* will change. Most people want outcomes but will not accept the changes they need to make in order to achieve those outcomes. They are stuck in their past and, what's more, they want you to stay there too. As much as people think they want the best for their friends and loved ones, the idea of someone close to them (or even associated with them) stepping away on a different path (even if they remain close) is frightening. Instead of supporting change, society will try to suppress it. To be successful, you will need to accept that change *will* happen—you will need to defend it and embrace it and be prepared (with your good thoughts) for resistance. You need to open yourself to winning.

Prepare for Success

During your journey, remember that many successful people started in the same position as you. It is a large, unexplored life bursting with opportunities. Open your mind and you open yourself to success.

I never thought life was fair.
I accepted the cards I was dealt
and found happiness my own way.
Then they said, "That's not fair,
you're always happy."

#FUKOFF (KINDLY)

(2)

LIFE ISN'T FAIR

Life's not easy. Don't try and make it that way. It's not fair, it never was, it isn't now, it won't ever be. Do not fall into the entitlement trap of feeling you are a victim, you are not. Get over it and get on with it.

MATTHEW MCCONAUGHEY

F THERE IS one universal truth that applies to all humankind, it is this: life isn't fair.

Some people are blessed with plenty, while others struggle to scrape by. Some of us are surrounded by love and support. Others are forced to deal with devastating circumstances—the sudden loss of a loved one, the trauma of rape, abuse, prejudice, or racism. For still others, the scars are of a subtler variety: bullies on the playground, the rejection of a parent. We are not all dealt the same hand at birth, nor do we have control over all our life experiences... **Life is not fair. It never was and never will be.**

It is also universally true that from this day forward, history is behind you. Whatever happened yesterday does not have to be what defines you today. You can choose to carry the love and the positive things that have happened in your life with you, and you can also choose to let go of the hurtful ones, to have hope, and, ultimately, to find success. In spite of where you come from, in spite of the immensity of your dreams or the barriers in your way, in spite of the limitations you face, there is nothing and no one that can stop you from seizing your dreams and achieving even more than you ever dared hope for—*if* you put your mind to it.

Easy? Not at all. Unfair? You bet. Achievable? In a heartbeat.

Ann, I Am Your Mother

I grew up knowing I was adopted. The second youngest in a family of girls, it was obvious from my skin tone that I was different from my sisters (how did that hen lay one brown egg and four white?). My Scottish/English parents, in all their academic and affluent glory, decided to adopt an Asian newborn into their already large family (when adopting Asian babies was unusual).

For the first half of my childhood, I tried to figure out why this was so significant. Why they fought about a decision they'd made so many years earlier. Why, in my father's fits of drunken rage, my name was wielded like a weapon between them. To be clear, when I say they fought, I mean it in a physical sense. My sisters and I witnessed relentless domestic violence growing up. Suffice to say, it was not a good upbringing and, apparently, I was the cause.

I have learned in life that if you wait long enough, the truth will reveal itself.

For me, the truth came knocking at the tender age of twelve. One day in the library of our Tudor home, my mother sat me down and divulged that she was, in fact, my biological mother (explains the cheekbones) and that I had another father; he was Hawaiian and an entertainer. *Period.* Not why she decided to tell me now. Not how this had happened. Just that I was not adopted and that she, after years of denying it, was my birth mother. She said it as matter-of-factly as one would chat about the weather, like she was checking off a to-do list:

"Ann, I'd like you to clean your room. Please take out the garbage—remember, it's raining, and . . . Oh, I am your biological mother."

And just like that, my world spun on a new axis.

There were two things I was certain of in that life-changing moment. One, I was extremely happy! I loved my mom and now, according to her, she was my blood relation. And two, my biological father must be none other than singer Don Ho, of "Tiny Bubbles" fame . . . Who else could it be? (Also, how cool is that?!)

"Anything else, Mom?"

"No."

"Okay, I'll take the garbage out."

**Success is getting what you want.
Happiness is wanting what you get.**

DALE CARNEGIE

The Don Ho Effect

We have all been "Don Ho-ed" to some extent in life. Moments such as when you find out your spouse has cheated and you start to rethink your entire history together—when you realize that what you thought was a fact was actually an assumption. When you remember everything from a different perspective: conversations, cellphones being taken into the bathroom, or your dowdy significant other suddenly booking a pedicure and tan (an abrupt decision to get a hair transplant or umbilical hernia repair is a slam dunk).

After the initial shock wears off, we try to make sense of these moments. We relive them, we overthink them, and we reinterpret them. Then we try to rationalize it all. We even question ourselves. How can facts have changed? Was it fake news, as President Trump loves to say, all along?

In my case, I realized that my existence, how I came into the world, was the catalyst for their arguments. I was the cause—living proof of a wife's infidelity that walked and talked alongside my adoptive father every day.

What I learned over a lifetime of reflection on my atypical parentage was that this was *their* problem, not mine. I did not cause the affair/conception/fake adoption. I did not insert myself into their lives (no pun intended) or choose them as my parents. In fact, I loved having them as my parents. (I just wished they'd stop fighting . . . and blaming it on my existence.) In short, I chose not to blame them. I chose to let them sort out their issues regarding the reason for my existence. And I chose not to overanalyze the circumstances surrounding it. The fact was, I would never really know why they acted the way they did (I can guess), nor could I change the outcome. *I could only change how I reacted to them.*

I'm not really sure how I came to this realization. I think I just evolved into it, accepting them and hoping they (eventually) would accept me (and calm down). It was *how* I became and then it was *who* I became. And, bless them, in all of it they *did* keep me, they *did* raise me, and they *did* love me... I just would have preferred my adopted dad's nose.

The Blame Game

Often, we look back on our childhood as the defining force of our future. The parents who raised us, attempted to raise us, or ruined us are credited with making us the person we are today. We draw from those early memories, moulding them into the answers for our accomplishments or the reasons for our struggles, and then we spend years trying to resurrect or erase those memories. Ultimately, we end up disappointed, because the past is inaccessible. We cannot step back in time or change our history; we can only change the lens through which we view it.

I chose not to dwell on my monumentally dysfunctional family and how growing up in that environment may have shaped me as an individual. For some people, it's not that easy. There are those who make a career out of blaming others. You know someone like this. I know someone like this. In our less than stellar moments, we may even *be* someone like this.

Here's how the blame game works: The "blamer" is always holding someone else responsible for their perceived failure. They blame their mother for not pushing them or not supporting them. They blame their partner for not wanting to spend more time with them. They blame the fact that they got pregnant when they didn't mean to, or that someone

"undeserving" got their dream job. It's always the fault of someone or something that they are not getting ahead.

The genius part of the blame game is that there is no end to who or what we can blame—the possibilities are endless! The economy is a mess! The weather ruined our event! The political climate is volatile! We can blame President Trump (he's crazy) or Hillary Clinton (she's a liar). Even our partner's sleep apnea can be at fault, if we're so inclined.

But there's one fact that the blame game conveniently ignores: When it comes to success, we really only ever have ourselves to blame. If other people, our personal life, the economy, or even the weather get in the way, the truth is, we didn't prepare for a change or respond to one when we should have. We blame the situation we are in instead of figuring out how best to manage it, how to change it, and how to learn from it. And, by so doing, we absolve ourselves of responsibility for our actions and our reactions.

There Are Two Types of People

Psychologists say there are only five types of people in the world. I think we can boil it down, in the simplest terms, to two: those who wait for opportunities to happen, and those who make opportunities happen.

The "If Onlys"

The first type waits for success to magically appear. They wait for that big investment tip that's going to change their life. They wait for Bitcoin to go the right way or, on the flip side, for "bad stuff" to stop happening to them. They dream of an "if" and an "if only." If only they had been born rich, if only they had married the right person, if only they had started sooner, done that, or said this. They don't reflect on an event or outcome they deem unfortunate and think, *How do I get to a place where I feel more fortunate in that area?* They think, *I'll be happy when*... and never truly are.

This type of person collects excuses the way some people (okay, *me*) collect designer shoes. They draw from past incidents in their life as the reason they have not found the success(es) they wanted. They may lament that they were adopted, or not adopted, or that their mother had an affair (and staged an elaborate fake adoption!). Whatever the case may be, they live their whole life blaming the past for the fact that they never get ahead.

The Doer

The second type of people are those who create their own opportunities for success. They don't look at their past as an obstacle. They envision where they want to be and take deliberate steps to achieve their goals—every day. They don't blame others or fixate on the challenges in their way. They look for opportunities in their ordeals, creating their own luck as opposed to looking for it. This type of person is a "doer." They are accountable for their actions and their decisions, and they get the job done.

The Third Type

Yes, yes, I know I said there are only two types. The third is really an amped-up version of the second—the doer who steps it up a notch. The doer who thinks big, takes risks, focuses their efforts, and commits to relentlessly, single-mindedly, wholeheartedly pursuing their goals. The third one is *How to Be Successful on Steroids*, minus actual steroids.

This last type—this is what excites me! This is what should excite you! It is what average, normal, everyday overachievers do. They envision a path, they face obstacles head-on, and they go for it. They put men on the moon, they start their own television station, they develop a revolutionary automobile in an existing (and saturated) market. That is, they dream big and they make magic happen.

Which One Are You?

Check one:

☐ If Only   ☐ Doer   ☐ Doer Plus

Now comes the tough question: which category do you want to fall into?

Being an *if only* is easy. We can stay stagnant and say, "Life sucks," or tell people they're "lucky" for the successes they achieve while bemoaning the sad state of our own affairs.

Or, we can be the change we seek. We can do the work, learn from our past, and find the solutions to whatever is getting in our way. Obviously, I'm going to argue that you want to be the second type of person—*the doer*. (The title of the book is *How to Be Successful*, after all.) If you aspire to be the amped-up version of the doer, all the better!

No One Said It Would Be Easy

Now don't get me wrong: I'm not saying it'll be easy. Life can be spectacularly unfair at times.

Crap happens. Sad things happen. Really, *really* sad things. When you get through the crap, when you can put it behind you, you have arguably survived it. But can you learn to not let it take you down with it? Can you learn to leave it in your past?

People don't. Too often, that "thing" that happened to them is the strike that sinks them.

I look back on where I came from, on the beatings I witnessed and those I took. On nursing wounds, my own and others', and learning to tiptoe so as not to ignite the ticking time bomb of my father's rage. I learned to help a drunk sit up and pat blood from his lips when I was ten, and how to pull a six-foot-five man off my mother when I was all of five feet. And eventually, I learned how to live with those memories and, more importantly, how to not make them my own. I didn't forget; I chose to leave them behind me.

I also learned that I'm not alone with my sad story. Whenever I tell someone about the traumatic events in my past, they inevitably volunteer their own stories of loss, of betrayal, of heartbreaking challenges, and, without fail, I am awed by their bravery. I realized that I am one of many who have had to not just survive but rise above painful events and experiences, and find happiness in spite of it all. And I learned that anyone can do it—at any age or stage of their life.

That crap—that full sack of crap—does not need to be the weight that drags you down.

When Crap Has Happened in Your Life

I have been asked why that stereotypical "Dad was an abusive alcoholic" or "_____ had an affair" or "I was abused" hasn't got in my way. The short answer is that I chose not to let it. I made a choice to move forward and leave my past where it belongs— behind me.

I grew up ducking blows and never quite understanding why the parents I loved acted the way they did. But I never judged them or questioned them about it. I didn't know any other life. I was powerless as a child, not having the tools or the experience to know how to get myself away from the abuse. But, for some reason, even then, I knew that other people's issues were not mine, even if those people were my parents. I worried for them. I was concerned about my mother's situation. But I knew that I was going to be okay.

The same cannot be said for my sisters. I've spent endless hours, days, months, then years over the course of my life at the bedsides of my sisters, in hospitals and in mental health institutes, struggling with the knowledge that they never recovered from our violent childhood. They were haunted by it, are haunted by it. And, in less generous moments, they resented the fact that I had been dealt a good gene card (thanks to the affair) and thereby escaped the ghosts of mental illness.

Why some of us are better equipped to withstand such horrors, I can't say. I do know it's our responsibility to ourselves to find a way, because no one can overcome our past for us. I also know that having a different biological father did not equip me with blinders or a pamphlet on how to survive abuse. I *chose* to move forward, and I still do.

At the end of the day, it's not what happened to you but what you choose to do with what you have experienced. It's how you move positively forward with the cards you were dealt that will form the foundation for a successful life. If you do not put the "things" that have happened behind you, if you do not acknowledge (to yourself), "This happened and I will not end up in that place again," you will never give yourself the opportunity to get over it. And if you do not start now, tomorrow will be the same—one more day of crap, and one more day to cry about.

We need to learn as much as we can from our past. We need to reflect on our experiences, heed the lessons they offer (even if all you learn is that you do not want to end up in that situation again), then move forward. If you don't, the past is going to hold your dreams hostage. The longer you dwell on negative events, the more time you invest licking the wounds of those past resentments, the longer they will keep you from creating the life you want. You'll be stuck in a "poor me" mindset, the one that keeps you in victim mode, absorbed by your insecurities and fixated on who or what is "to blame," and you will never achieve the life you desire and deserve. And believe me, you deserve so much more.

Getting Rid of Baggage

When you truly understand the cause of your negative thinking and the outcome of the [insert major challenging life incident here], you may choose to forgive the parties involved. Or you may decide "this person is not contributing positively to my life and there is nothing I can do about them." The next step, the one that will put you on more solid footing, is to take measures to surround yourself with people who do not stir that same emotion. We'll talk more in chapter 8 about the people you should keep in your life and those you s hould not.

Just know now that you're not going to get very far down the path to success if you keep lugging around the heavy baggage of your past. This does not mean denying it is there; it means you don't take it with you. Leave that bag "unclaimed" on the luggage carousel. While you're at it, you can go ahead and leave the blame behind as well. If you think *my life is not good* or even *I got myself into this*, know that there is a way to get yourself out of it. Stop blaming how you got here. You're here. Now let's see where else you can go.

> **You are not the victim of circumstance, but the creator of opportunity.**
>
> ANN KAPLAN

Adversity Is the Door to Opportunity

Adversity, like grey hair and taxes, is unavoidable. Yet, when faced with it, our first reaction is often to hide. Or at least to try to hide (see: unavoidable). It is common for us to see problems and challenges as barriers, and sometimes those barriers seem so insurmountable that we give up. It is also common, however, for people to find a way to lift those barriers if they so desire. Adversity brings opportunities—opportunities to learn about ourselves, opportunities to grow, opportunities to forge new paths. In the words of Albert Einstein, "Adversity introduces a man to himself."

Some people make enormous sums off an economic slump. Some view a sudden loss of employment as the end of a way of life while others see it as offering a clean slate and a fresh new beginning. Adversity can be the straw that breaks us, or it can be the forge that hardens our resolve and empowers us with the knowledge that we can not only survive but overcome any hardship.

Howard Schultz, the mastermind behind Starbucks, grew up in a subsidized housing complex for the poor and went on to build the biggest coffee house chain in the world. British physicist Stephen Hawking was diagnosed with motor neurone disease at age twenty-one, and was eventually confined to a wheelchair and rendered unable to speak unaided. In spite of these overwhelming challenges, he went on to become world-renowned for his groundbreaking research and prize insights into cosmology, time, and space. Wherever there is adversity, there is possibility. Adversity is only limiting if you allow it to be.

Life Lessons from Adversity

The adversity I experienced growing up gave me the opportunity to invite change into my life, to know that I do not want the tragedy or pain that adversity brought me. And it continues to shape me. I may sit and cry when adversity first strikes, but I always face it, knowing that moving forward gives me the power to create a better future, to come out the other side stronger.

- **Adversity allows me to rethink my life.** If I learn from what has happened, I will be empowered to rise above all else.

- **Adversity is a wake-up call.** If I am ignoring the signs, if I am being too safe, then adversity will find me. What I have done in the past does not determine what I can achieve in the future. I need to live. I need to let adversity allow me to understand and achieve more.

- **I can look at adversity and feel only the pain, or I can turn adversity into a positive thing.** I must see adversity as opportunity, as amazing—as the best thing that ever happened to me.

- **Lastly, adversity has allowed me to refocus my life.** If and when I am faced with adversity, I now know that I can learn from it (if I choose to, and I always do) and I can come out stronger.

(My father would be proud. At least one of them . . .)

Adversity will always knock on our doors, but it is with the knowledge that we have the power to learn from it and move forward that we gain the strength to overcome, and even thrive, in times of adversity.

Strength does not come from what you can do, it comes from overcoming the things you thought you once couldn't.

RIKKI ROGERS

But What If Good Things Happened in My Past?

Now, you might not like to hear this, but ruminating on your past achievements can be just as detrimental as rehashing negative events. If you try to coast along on a win, or an award, or even a "dream job" or educational degree, assuming that those wins will continue to happen without your effort, your success will stagnate. You'll find yourself boring people at cocktail parties with tales of "that time when . . ." or you'll notice that, four years out, people are still introducing you as "the valedictorian in grade six/high school/university." Those successes are as good as behind you; dwelling on them keeps you stuck in the past.

Instead, think of your past wins as trophies on your desk— validation that you're heading in the right direction, but yesterday's news. Sure, it was an accomplishment and it may have opened doors for you. But you cannot rely on that trophy to continue to open other doors. Your past wins are opportunities to learn from and to leverage in order to bring you closer to the life you desire.

But, But, But . . .

No *but*s. Life is hard . . . *really* hard. Crap happens, get over it. Great things happen, enjoy the moment, and then look toward your next move. Learn from your experiences and don't let them hold you back. Period.

Back to My Birth Father

Five years after the "disclosure" of the truth about my birth, I found out that my father was *not* Don Ho (surprise, surprise) but an entertainer named Berne 'Hal-Mann. I cannot say I was pleased about that discovery. By then, I'd flown to Hawaii a few times to see Don Ho perform, sitting in the audience thinking, *There's my dad! The tall, handsome, "Tiny Bubbles" guy!* Then he wasn't. When I found out the true identity of bio-dad—a celebrity not quite as famous or as tall as Don Ho—I immediately booked a flight to Hawaii and set out on a mission to meet him. I did ... but that's a story for another day.

Afterwards, I spent many years trying to get to know the man responsible for my conception, trying to find acceptance or an understanding of why I even existed. I was looking for that "perfect father," someone who would love me unconditionally. I wanted that knight in shining armour and, damn it, my father was the chosen one.

But each time I flew to Hawaii, he was busy. He moved to another island. He'd make promises to visit and then not follow through. There were times I found myself standing in the Honolulu airport, tears running down my cheeks, with the dawning realization that he was not getting off the plane. "Sorry, I couldn't make it this time." I'd tell myself it didn't matter. That next time he would show up. Next time he'd tell me he loved me—after all, he was my dad. But next time always turned out to be more of the same.

I had almost given up on him when one beautiful day in Waikiki (disclaimer: every day is beautiful in Waikiki) I was Don Ho-ed a second time.

I was in my forties. Decades had passed, and I had accepted my biological father's position in my life. On this day, Berne had (finally) flown over from the Big Island to visit. By coincidence, I was staying at the Hilton Hawaiian Village, the very place where he used to perform and had met my mother. (His picture hangs in the hotel to this day.) We were standing on the balcony of the second-floor pool of the Ali'i Tower, overlooking the Hilton Hawaiian Village, as dusk approached. It was a surreal moment in a surreal setting, and after years of hope my biological father looked at me and, in all tenderness, said, "There is something I have to tell you."

Tears welled up in my eyes, and I looked away. This was the moment when he would tell me he loved me. This was the moment my father would validate my existence. This was the moment I had waited for my entire life.

I turned to him expectantly. "Yes?"

Berne leaned in and whispered with a conspiring wink, "Your mother was a screamer!"

Like I said, life isn't fair. It is often ridiculous, though.

· ·

Life is not fair. It's just fairer than death, that's all.

WILLIAM GOLDMAN

· ·

EXERCISE 2: The Steps to Change

Life may not have been fair to you, but you can give it (and yourself) the opportunity to start afresh.

Step 1: Change must happen. When you are not in a job/career or position that you are happy with, when you want more than your current circumstances offer, when you look at yourself and feel you could be a better person, you know that you need to make a change (or ten). That simple thought is the first step toward realizing the future you seek. Write down what you want in life. What does your ideal future look like?

Step 2: Understand that only you can change your life. No one else can make the changes for you. You are fully dependent on your own decision making. To get through this step (in thinking and in process) you must accept that it is fully and unequivocally up to you and you alone. What are you going to do to bring about these changes?

Step 3: Believe that change is possible. If you believe that you have the power to find success, if you believe that by taking calculated steps you will be able to achieve the change you want, that the efforts put in today will enable the change tomorrow, you can achieve anything you set your mind to. But first, you must *believe*. Believe it is possible and it will be possible.

I can control anything.
I was called ugly, I bought implants.
I was called stupid, I got a doctorate.
I was called a bitch, I said,
"You're right . . . and I like
me the way I am."

(3)

CREATE YOUR REALITY

**Thoughts are the greatest vehicles to change, power,
and success. Everything begins with a thought.**

OPRAH WINFREY

ONE FALL EVENING not long after 9/11, Stephen, my
now-husband, and I were at the Rainbow Room in New
York City. At the time, we had been dating for a few
years and I felt certain he was on the brink of proposing. Sure
enough, that night at dinner, in the middle of our meal, Stephen got down on one knee and pulled out a small velvet
box. Everyone in the restaurant was watching as the scene
unfolded. Tears came to my eyes as I took the box from him
and opened it. Inside was a Supergirl ring—a cheap painted
metal ring.

Stephen looked at me and said, "I think you are a super girl."
Then he sat down and finished his meal.

To say I was disappointed by the turn of events that evening would be a gross understatement. I spent the rest of dinner, head down, tears dripping onto my plate. I cried on the way back to the hotel and continued to sob sporadically throughout the night. (Related aside: not every story I tell you in this book is going to end with me crying. Just FYI.) The next day, on the plane home (I'd more or less composed myself by then), I looked over at Stephen, he was smiling, and again I turned my head away and started to get weepy. What he said next made me acutely aware that I was living in a completely different reality from him.

Stephen looked at the tears streaming down my face and said, "I can't believe how happy you are!" And he went back to reading his paper.

I never corrected Stephen. I can tell you that he proposed "for real" three months later.

There Are No True Facts

Is Stephen obtuse when it comes to reading social cues? Probably. But he's not alone. Each of us sees the world through the filter of our experiences and our emotions, and we make that interpretation our reality. It's why some people see the glass as half empty while for others it's half full; it's why we jump to irrational conclusions about people we've never met; it's probably how "emo" became a thing, but that last one is neither here nor there.

The point is that we can be in the same place, at the same time, and see the same things, and yet take away completely different experiences. For instance, if you put five people in a room with a clown for ten minutes, you'll get five very different reports on the show. If you are a fan of magic, you may focus on his card trick prowess and be delighted by his deft sleight of hand. If you're into cosmetics, you'll pay close attention to his costume and makeup and judge his performance based on the quality of its execution. If you have coulrophobia (a fear of clowns), the experience will be anxiety inducing, the minutes agonizingly slow.

One person's truth will never be the same as another's, yet neither can be proven false. We live in our own reality—very real to each of us, but almost entirely of our own creation. When it comes to perception, there are no true facts.

Which brings us to this . . .

Reality Check

Nowhere is the impact of perception more poignant than in the storyline you create for yourself.

Your life is not a Wikipedia page of facts and important events, verified with supporting links. It's not the sum of the 150 characters in your Instagram bio or the clever handle on your Twitter account. The story of your life is determined by the way you internally integrate events and experiences—how you break them down, interpret them, and reshape them in your mind into the story of "you." That narrative becomes your identity. So what are you keeping in your story?

Too often we dream of achievement and then do the one thing guaranteed to stifle it before we even get started. It's called a "reality check." We squash our dream, not because we didn't try, but because we told ourselves we couldn't achieve it. When, *in reality*, anything is possible if you can imagine it.

And that, right there, is the difference between people who realize incredible success and fortune and you. What did Pat Gallant-Charette do to swim across the English Channel at sixty-six years of age? What would two men with a bicycle shop have done on that cool December day in 1903 if they'd said, "Get real, man can't fly"? The thing that sets Orville and Wilbur Wright apart from the rest of the world is that they imagined doing something that no one had ever done—they made a perceived impossibility a reality. And so can you.

The Truth Will Set You Free

Once you accept that you live in your own reality, three things will come into sharp focus:

1. **You will see the world differently.** When you understand that you live in your own reality, you will view the world through the lens of your experience. You will become more aware of and open to different points of view, and you will stop seeing everything as a fact. You may even find yourself taking the initiative to understand differing perspectives.

2. **You will take control of your reality.** If you accept that we all live in our own reality, then you can also accept that you are in control of your reality, that you determine your unique perspective on life and how you live it, and that how you spend every moment is a choice.

   If you choose to live a healthy lifestyle, regular exercise and nutritious food will be your reality. If you choose to live a life of learning or to wake up happy every day, books and ideas and gratitude will become your reality. If you choose to turn your home into a cat sanctuary or to live out your dream of becoming an anime character, you can make that your reality too. How you live your life is entirely up to you.

3. **You'll realize that no one has greater influence over your reality than you.** Since you, and no one else, are the creator of your reality, it's up to you to make it uniquely yours. Don't follow what others believe in, don't live someone else's dream or idea of what reality should be—craft your own. You can model your reality after people you admire, you can look to them for inspiration and guidance, but their path will not be yours. It's not for you to compare or to concern yourself with others. Creating your reality is an inside job, and it manifests in your every decision, thought, and action. It's taking control of the path you are on.

It's entirely in your power to make success your reality!

> My general attitude to life is to enjoy
> every minute of every day. I never do anything with
> a feeling of, "Oh God, I've got to do this today."
>
> RICHARD BRANSON

Help! I'd Rather Have Richard Branson's Reality

I mean, don't we all? Richard Branson has launched a space company and kite-surfed across the English Channel. He owns an entire island in the British Virgin Islands and skydives with the Obamas. His reality looks awesome!

But the most impressive part of Branson's life is not the trappings of wealth that surround it. It's not even his enviable mane of hair. It's how authentic it feels to Branson. Billionaire bank account aside, he's built a life that embodies the ideals he holds dear: philanthropy, adventure, and fun! And he lives it with unapologetic enthusiasm.

The Bransons of the world show us that our dreams are possible and that we can create not only the lives we imagine but ones that exceed our wildest dreams.

You Are What You Think

My imagination has always kept me going. I imagine myself in a position—getting parts, being on shows, writing a book (even one where I absolutely feel I know nothing about the subject!)—and I know I can make it happen. If I can see myself doing it, I know I can achieve it. Any successful person will tell you that half of accomplishing any goal is simply believing you can do it.

Try it. Think of a goal you want to achieve and envision how you would look if it came to pass—what you would do, how you would conduct yourself, what you would hope to accomplish. It's all right if you can't see the whole path. Few of us do. Oprah Winfrey didn't imagine when she was fourteen and pregnant that she'd one day be named the most powerful celebrity by *Forbes* magazine. She *did* imagine she could live a better life. Maybe you can only envision the next step or two along that path. That's okay. The important thing is that you start heading in the right direction, or even just start looking in the right direction!

Because if you can start to visualize yourself doing something, you can find a way to achieve it.

You Are the Narrator of Your Reality

If you read that last line and then immediately thought, *But can I?* You're not alone. One of the biggest barriers we'll encounter on the path to success is self-doubt—that little voice whispering in your ear, *Who do you think you are? You're not smart or good enough to achieve that. You're too old/too young.* Left unchecked, that voice can spiral out of control, spinning a self-defeating monologue of negativity that will leak into all aspects of your life. *You married the wrong person. What if this isn't the right career for me? This is too hard.*

Stop.

The battle you face in your head will be the most challenging one to conquer; there is no greater pain than that inflicted by an internal enemy. You may not know how you will get somewhere, but knowing that you are in control and capable of getting through something, *anything*, is within you.

What's important here, the thing we need to pay attention to, is how our internal biases shape our reality. How our past experiences, prejudices, and expectations colour our perception and influence our thoughts. Because here's the thing: our perceptions determine our reality, but our thoughts aren't actually real.

Every feeling, sensation, or idea that pops into your awareness happens only within the confines of your mind. It's an experience exclusive to you, neither heard nor experienced by anyone else. What makes a thought *feel* real is the consideration we give to it. By focusing on a thought, we breathe life into it. We relate to it as if that thought were an event occurring in the "real world," when in fact it has no impact whatsoever on the thing we're thinking about unless we pair it with an action. A thought is merely a manifestation of your mind. If we choose not to ponder it—*poof!*—that thought ceases to exist.

How liberating is that?! You can choose which thoughts you give attention to, which ones enter the realm of your reality.

Change Your Programming

So, we've established the entirely unsurprising fact that our thoughts are not always positive. We all have doubts, negative ruminations, even demons lurking in our minds. *Even Richard Branson and Oprah Winfrey.* That inner voice always ready to weigh in with *That person would never find me interesting/ attractive* or *They will never hire me.* To keep things exciting, these self-defeating thoughts are especially prone to flood our brain when we're at our most stressed, vulnerable, and/or weak. Inner critics are fun like that.

Forget it, I could never achieve that.

To shunt these negative thoughts to the side, or, better yet, to choke the life out of them with the brute strength of our positivity, we have to understand what is causing them in the first place. What made us fast-forward to a negative assumption? Why did we feel that someone would not find us interesting? Or employable? Why did we admit defeat before we'd even tried?

Part of the answer lies in your inner programming. Your current beliefs about love, money, health, success, self-worth, happiness, and just about everything in between are stored in your subconscious mind and are likely the same ones you held when you were ten. So you can go ahead and blame your parents for any self-defeating beliefs you might be clinging to. (Just kidding.) It is true that our identity and who we become in the world is contingent upon our subconscious programming.

The subconscious mind is a massive memory-storage unit with virtually unlimited space that stores and recalls memory so you don't have to keep relearning the same things over and over again each day. Current wisdom suggests that most of our subconscious programming happens before the age of eight, when we're human sponges absorbing and storing everything the adults around us are doing, feeling, and saying in order to figure out how to function in the world. This information becomes the blueprint for our habits, beliefs, memories, learning, and physiological processes.

So if your mom told you things like, "If you chew your nails, they'll grow into claws in your stomach!" or taught you to make a two-inch-thick seat cover out of toilet paper before using a public toilet when you were a kid, the grown-up you might have concerns about germs that aren't based entirely on reality.

The other part of the equation is that these beliefs are reinforced by our nervous system. Humans are creatures of habit. We experience stress and light up a cigarette or chew our lips/

hair/nails. We hear slow, ominous music during a movie and we cover our eyes. We infer what is going to happen and subconsciously respond. When that response matches the perceived cue, we are biochemically rewarded with a dose of dopamine,[2] the "feel-good hormone," which thereby reinforces our reaction.

To change our thought habits, we must consciously acquire new ideas and thoughts and let them permeate our subconscious until they become beliefs. In other words, we need to rewire our thinking. To do that, we must become aware of when we are falling into these negative patterns and what triggers them in the first place, so we can replace these faulty lines of logic with more positive patterns of thought. Easy peasy, right? Let's work on that!

1. Rephrase Your Habitual Thoughts

Inner doubts are merely learned scripts. *I'm stupid, I'm boring, I'll never figure out how to accessorize*—these are false limits we impose upon ourselves. Most of the time, these words don't apply. You don't arrive at a dinner party with these negative labels tattooed on your forehead. The only person assigning them to you is that pesky inner critic.

There is no reason you can't feel intelligent or interesting or wildly successful! But first you have to get a handle on the negative self-talk. Start by replacing limiting thoughts with positive phrases. For example:

- Replace *I'm unattractive* with *I am a unique individual.*
- Replace *I'm odd* with *I am interesting.*
- Replace *I'm boring* with *I am permitted to converse about topics that interest me.*

---

2   engineeringandleadership.com/change-inner-negative-narrative/

Use positive phrases and they'll become self-fulfilling prophecies. And remember, no one is judging whether or not you are cool enough in life. (If they are, know that they've got bigger problems you probably shouldn't concern yourself with.) When you learn to control and direct your mind, distancing yourself from negative thoughts, you can teach that inner monologue to work for you, not against you. Teach it well enough and your inner voice can be your biggest champion.

2. Set Intentions for Yourself

An intention, known more colloquially as a prayer, is an expression of a hope or wish. Like buying a lottery ticket, it sparks your imagination to consider what you desire, and then repeats it to your subconscious mind. Unlike the spectacularly low probability of actually winning the lottery, simply expressing your desire brings you infinitely closer to achieving it. The best part about intentions, prayers, or whatever you want to call them is that you can express them anywhere and you don't even need to say them out loud. I could be praying right now that you love this book so much you'll go out and buy a copy for all your friends, and you'd be none the wiser. (*Whispers to self: please love this book and buy it for all your friends . . .*)

3. Expose Yourself to Positive Thinking

When we are in self-help mode and are looking to improve our lives, we read books, blogs, and stories that lift us up and put us in a hopeful and positive mindset. How many times have you been moved by the grand achievements of an underdog, or felt your eyes fill with tears before a selfless act of generosity? When we actively seek that which is positive, we provoke positive thoughts. And that feels good! The same is true for flowers, puppies, and babies. (My oldest biological son, Barrett, was a notable exception. He looked like ET on a good day.) Thinking of happy things makes us feel happy.

Why wait? The more you expose yourself to positive thoughts, ideas, and people, the more positivity you'll invite into life and your reality. Consciously start the morning on an uplifting note and you'll carry that with you throughout the day. (Even if some days that positive note means simply getting out of bed and into the shower.)

4. Visualize Your Way to Success

You've heard visualization touted as a tool of success. There's also a high likelihood you tried it for a minute and quickly forgot about it, rolled your eyes, and/or dismissed it altogether. But there's a good reason why it keeps coming up in life advice columns. Research shows that the subconscious mind does not distinguish between actual experiences and imagined ones. That is, visualizing a goal being accomplished creates the same mental instructions as physically accomplishing it.

This can be a particularly useful tool when we have to prepare for a new undertaking and anxiety is getting the best of us. In these instances, visualization has been found to enhance motivation, increase confidence, improve performance, and increase states of flow. It will literally rewire your brain toward achieving your best life.

The key to effective visualization is to be as specific as possible in your mental imagery. What does achieving your goal look like? How does it feel? How will you act? Imagine watching yourself achieve the goal, then switch perspectives and see the events unfolding through your own eyes as your goal is achieved. Imagine obstacles that might pop up along the way as well and how you'll tackle them. Critical visualization can be a powerful motivator and help drive you to keep pushing yourself to new heights.

Believe in Yourself

To change your reality, you only need to change your perception of what reality is. If you believe you will never make money, you won't. If you believe you can never get in shape, you will continue to be out of shape. If you think you are worthless, you will *feel* worthless, and if you believe that your health and well-being are simply the result of genetics or the environment you live in, if you believe there is nothing you can do to improve, you will stay on the path you've always been on.

Believe it will not happen and it won't. But dream a little dream, find faith in yourself, and the world will be waiting for you. Your reality is limited only by what you believe to be true. So go ahead and imagine the best possible life for yourself—a life without any of the barriers currently in your way. Envision who you want to be and take steps to become that person. (And if you want to steal Richard Branson's island idea, by all means do so. Johnny Depp did.)

What Is It about Weddings in Our Family . . . ?

We started this chapter talking about an event that precluded my wedding. I'm going to end it on a more recent wedding in our family.

A few years ago I was invited to celebrate my younger brother's nuptials in Cancún. Brandon was (at last count) the twelfth child of our biological father. (Berne played women like he played keyboards, procreating his way through the 1950s, '60s, and '70s via a few too many marriages and several more paramours, all of whom he conveniently dubbed "babe.")

Brandon was marrying a beautiful redhead from Omaha, Nebraska. Her Catholic parents had come to know my brother as "an only child," apparently unaware of his siblings scattered across the continent. (I get it. I mean, the conversation never likely opened up with, "Hey, Berne, do you have eleven other children?") During the ceremony, an intimate affair in a beachfront chapel, I couldn't help but notice the perplexed looks on the faces of my brother's future in-laws. It was a look that said, "Where in the world did this (Hawaiian) Von Trapp family come from?!" I wondered, was Brandon just going to spring it on them after the nuptials that our father might need to stay in the confessional for a few hours, if not days?

At the reception, the disparity between our two families was even more pronounced. Brandon's Hawaiian relations, about seven of his siblings, had flown in for the wedding, and were singing, dancing, and playing piano; performing is in our father's DNA, and it's in ours as well. The Nebraska contingent were a more reserved bunch, taking in the scene, slack jawed, from their tables.

After tearful toasts to the bride, to the bridesmaids, and lastly to the mothers, one after the other crying their way through the well-wishes, the MC held up a glass and asked, "Does anyone else have something to say?"

We all know that this is a moment when the best thing to do is to shut up. Asking this question is just a formality; rarely is the betrothed couple hoping for a few unplanned words from the crowd. But someone had to address the elephant in the room.

I stood up (having had a few glasses of wine) and declared, "I have an announcement!"

The room fell silent. The only sound the waves lapping the banks of the Mayan Riviera.

"I have an announcement," I continued, as I waved a Mexican waiter over.

I looked at my new sister-in-law and welcomed her to the extended family, then said, "I would also like to welcome another person," putting my arm around the waiter I had just summoned to my side. "Pablo here is joining us today, as he is the thirteenth child of our father, Berne."

What happened next floored me . . .

Not only did my brother's new family believe me, *our* family did. My father was seconds away from getting up and yelling, "Son!" (Pablo, for his part, just stood there smiling, not understanding a word I was saying.) For a few confused moments the preconceived notions of everyone in that room came up against a different version of reality.

Then the room burst into laughter. The elephant left the room. My father, to this day, is still wondering if Pablo is his progeny.

Reality is what you make it.

EXERCISE 3: Rewrite Your Rules

Are you living by an outdated list of rules? Often we restrict ourselves to limiting beliefs that are entirely of our own creation. We think things like, *Oh, I could never do that/be that/*

get away with wearing that. Give yourself permission to rewrite your rules. Think about times when you have been uncomfortable or experienced self-doubt and consider what rule you can incorporate to change how you think. Remember, the rules you have previously imposed are arbitrary and can be altered. Start a new list!

An example (for me) would be:

- Clothing: I will dress how I please.
- Being a nerd: I am allowed to be different.
- Negative people: I do not have to respond to questions set up to judge me.
- Social media: I will post who I am, not what I'm told to be.
- Changing my mind: I am allowed to have a different opinion.

Be creative! Give yourself permission to be the person you would like to be. You may still doubt yourself, you may still hesitate, but you can look to your rules for guidance and empower yourself to live by your own guidelines.

(II)

THE SIX PRINCIPLES OF SUCCESS

You can ask me to do anything—
to help, to give, to love,
even to work harder.
Just don't ask me to be less
of a person than I am.

(4)

LIVE YOUR PURPOSE

**Try not to become a man
of success, but a man of value.**

ALBERT EINSTEIN

IN MY EARLY teens, I embarked on a tour of accidental enlightenment. While other kids my age were going to the movies and on dates, I went to workshops put on by Deepak Chopra, Swami Muktananda, and later his daughter, Chidvilasananda. I took in teachings of Bhagwan Shree Rajneesh and dined at fast-food restaurants with Deva Magdalena. (For the record, I've never liked fast food. I did enjoy when she picked up the bill.) During my time at home, I attended the United Church, taking in Christmas and Easter Mass with my family.

In those formative years, the thing that stood out most for me was the number of people looking to find answers, wanting to fix "things." There'd be hundreds of us packed into hotel

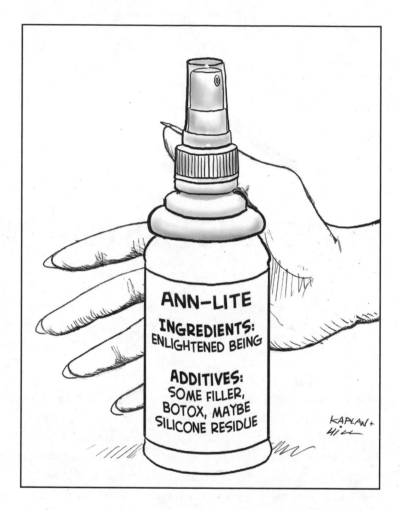

conference rooms in Hawaii to learn from Deepak and other spiritual teachers. We'd line up in sweaty auditoriums, attempting to sit comfortably on the floor while we chanted "*om namah shivaya*" without even knowing what it meant (at least for me). I'd listen, every now and then peeking (with my one eye) to see if everyone else was paying attention... they always were... *sway, sway*.

I was skeptical in the beginning, to say the least. The teachings never seemed to contradict one another, unless they were talking about a particular "god" or "being." The universal goal was to find your "enlightened" self. (Why does that word always drum up a slimmer version of oneself? "This is my friend Ann-Lite"—same person, less emotional baggage!)

Why, I wondered, is everyone looking for answers? Why can't they just be good and not attend all these workshops? Why are they looking to fix their broken pasts? Then the obvious: why make mistakes in the first place, only to have to go back to fix them . . . or be forgiven later?

I would leave each talk perplexed as to what it was I was supposed to be understanding, although there was always a take-away, always an interesting way to present thought. And I was invariably thankful that I had been there, not realizing the impact these teachings would have on my life, throughout my life.

It was in one of these early workshops that a few people divulged that they felt I was, in fact, "enlightened." This was funny because a) I was sixteen and b) I rarely said anything at these events. I did not criticize or agree, I just observed. I guess this made me (appear) enlightened? Kind of like Chance the gardener, the Peter Sellers character in the movie *Being There*. He said nothing, referenced his days as a gardener—"As long as the roots are not severed, all is well. And all will be well in the garden"—and was soon whisked off to run for the highest office in America. "Brilliant," so the movie goes, "he was brilliant."

A lot can be said for doing nothing, it seems.

So, knowing how human and confused and supposedly "enlightened" I was, and seeing the uncertainty on face after face, I had an overwhelming desire to find hope and find myself. In short, I was hooked.

The First Principle

My spiritual awakening didn't end with adolescence. Over the years, I've chanted with the Dalai Lama Buddhists in the temple near Lake Como, my sky-high heels neatly tucked at the back of the room amongst the flip-flops and thong sandals (some things never change...). I later studied spirituality at PhD level, and recently I became an ordained minister (neither one requires me to take my shoes off). Suffice it to say, spirituality has been a shaping force throughout my life.

But I also embrace the notion that these beliefs are deeply personal. So rest assured, this isn't the part of the book where I attempt to indoctrinate you into a specific set of spiritual beliefs. I'm not even going to tell you my own, at least not at length. Nor is this book about "how to be a good person," though I personally believe we should all aspire to that. This book is about living a life of success. To do that, you must develop a set of core values, values that will be the moral compass guiding all your decisions, because without them you will have a difficult time making *any* decision, let alone the right one.

That's why the first guiding principle on the path to success is spirituality—or, if you prefer, *moral intelligence*.

Now, you might say...

But I Am Not Spiritual

We are not talking a transcendental awakening here. If you feel you are not spiritual, read on. If you feel you don't want to follow a predetermined belief set, don't. But learning about those of others, their spiritual journey, their religion, and what has helped them find their purpose, can help you define a set of values that work for you.

I believe my study of spirituality has opened my mind toward the need, as a whole person, to be acutely aware of my core values, to work toward bettering myself, and to use the spiritual disciplines I accept to guide me through life. I believe those workshops helped me realize how ordinary I am, and that when my thinking goes in one direction, I am the one who can bring it back on track, using my learnings and awareness to guide me.

In many ways, the pursuit of spiritual knowledge is a science, a formula that creates a predictable outcome. Good in, good out. Knowledge and awareness in, compassion out. Et cetera. It is a lot easier to believe in science than to believe there is a God driving us. After all, we can control science by understanding it...

So, fear not, you don't have to be spiritual, you don't have to move into a Volkswagen van on Salt Spring Island, and you don't have to give up beer. You don't even have to label it "spirituality." You do need to identify your core values. Let's do that!

- -

Your beliefs become your thoughts, your thoughts become your words, your words become your actions, your actions become your habits, your habits become your values, your values become your destiny.

MAHATMA GANDHI

- -

Your Value Statement

Your values are the essence of who you are. The values you embody will be what people unconsciously associate with you. The simple act of wanting to be a better person, of striving to become aware of who you want to be, is a step toward embodying self-awareness.

The second step is defining the values that are important to you. What do you value in yourself? What qualities do you value in life, in others? Do you place a premium on honesty and ethics? Do you feel it's important to serve your community, or is providing a stable foundation for your family a top priority? Do you value adventure and personal growth? Or does maintaining a certain level of stability and contentment take precedence? Defining these values will enable you to build a life based on the ideals you hold dear.

How Do I Find My Values?

When I first thought to look for my purpose in life, I asked myself, why am I here? For some people, the answer is procreation. They believe we are here to put children on this earth or to make it a better place by raising good citizens. (I have eight children, so maybe there's something to that.) But I've always felt there must be more to it than just populating the planet (enjoyable as that is).

In seeking the "why," I also sought a set of values I would live by. I didn't want to sit at the deathbeds of my parents, telling them I loved them and apologizing for taking the Volvo for a joyride when I was thirteen. I wanted to be able to say to myself that I gave love, that at every opportunity I gave them a good daughter, that I thanked them for giving me life, and that, in all of their flaws or perceived mistakes, I did not judge them—I offered only gratitude. And I think I did. When I lost my dad and later my mother—both endured drawn-out health issues—I felt that I gave them all I could, and I take comfort in that to this day.

For me, family is my highest priority. They are what gives my life and work meaning and purpose; everything else trickles down from there. When I consider a new venture, whether it's a new business or a new show, my first thought is, *Does this serve my family and, if it will require travel, is it worth the time that will be taken away from them?* This extends to my work family as well: I weigh every major business decision based on how it will affect the people who work for me. By keeping that value in sharp focus in my mind, it becomes easy not only to make the right decisions but to feel confident about those decisions.

The Values Argument

Here comes the twist: who's to say which values are right?

Just as no two people are the same, there is no one correct belief system. Where you feel you have good strong values, the person sitting across from you could have a completely different but equally strong set of values, based on a different upbringing and mindset. And sometimes those belief systems will be in conflict. One person's most cherished and fundamental core values could be in direct opposition to yours. (Views on abortion, the death penalty, and same-sex marriage are polarizing examples of this.)

You do not have to agree, or disagree, with any standpoint, but you should accept that these differences exist and, more importantly, that we're all entitled to have them. Question, inquire, read, and learn about the values you hold. But also investigate those you don't agree with. Understanding the beliefs of others, religious or otherwise, will give you insight into who they are and, ultimately, into yourself.

Remember, it's not for us to say whose values are good and whose values are not. The truth is, there is no one "right" set of values.

Except mine.

(Just kidding.)

Predictable Things That Happen When You Live Your Core Values

When you use your core values to guide your decisions and actions, you'll find you are living life without asking for forgiveness, being accountable for your actions, and not jumping into judgment of others. (Maybe I do share my core values after all . . .). A number of things will automatically manifest in your life:

- **Decision making will be easier.** When you draw from a value set upon which to base your decisions, it's like pulling an answer from a reference library. You always know the answer . . .

- **You will become more dependable.** A by-product of living your core values is that you will become predictable and consistent in your decisions and actions. When you live your values, you cannot be bought or swayed, your heart will be open, and you will live without regretting the choices you make.

- **You'll feel more fulfilled.** Values imbue your life with purpose. When your life and work align with your core values, you'll feel you are living your authentic self—and it's incredibly fulfilling!

- **You'll feel motivated.** Grounded in your purpose, your core values will give you a powerful and lasting source of motivation. You'll be focused on the road ahead and excited about where the journey is taking you, confident that choices you make are leading you in the right direction.

- **You'll be empowered to fight bad habits.** Your core values will keep you on track. If health is one of your core values, you will commit to cultivating your physical health. You'll pay attention to how different foods and activities make you feel, and you won't want foods that don't serve your body.

- **Your life will shift in amazing ways.** Your core values will intuitively point you in the right direction. If you continue down that path, your life will move toward embodying all that you desire and hold dear.

- **You'll sprout angel wings.** (But only in your mind.)

It Won't Happen Overnight

Sounds miraculous, right? When you start living your core values, the path to your purpose will unfold before you. That doesn't mean there won't be moments when things go off track. We all feel pangs of uncertainty when someone is critical of us. We all have moments when we wish we had someone else's lifestyle (or even life) or when we wish we had handled a situation differently. By checking in with our core values, we can

"I AM TRYING TO FIND MYSELF".

learn from all of it. We can self-evaluate and take the lessons with us, allowing these lessons to assist in future decisions. You don't give yourself the cop-out excuse "to err is human," but rather you say to yourself, "Because I am human, I have the ability to learn from my mistakes."

And that's the beauty of it. If you don't like yourself, if you find something about your actions that you are uncomfortable with, your core values will empower you to change. And guess what?

It will just click.

At some point in the not so distant future, you'll look back and say, "Hey, I survived that and I came out okay." You'll look in the mirror and like who you see. What's more, when you get there, people will like the person they find. You will be a person of value. Funny thing is, you always were (a person of value, that is), you just didn't realize it.

> ## Success is living your life the way you want to.
>
> ANN KAPLAN

Do I Need to Share My Values?

Yes. But only with yourself.

Owning your beliefs doesn't mean you have to broadcast them. I may have studied spirituality, but my spiritual beliefs are my own. When you have strong values, you don't have to discuss or defend them. Your values are your own, and whether you decide to share your purpose or not is entirely up to you. What's important is that you live by your values. When you do that, your values will be naturally expressed in your actions and your words.

Love Is All There Is

There is only one physical sign in my home, and it says, *Love is all there is*. That sign is based on something a wise person once told me: if you are ever in doubt about what to do, about how to respond, then "give love." I hold this saying in my mind when I am wondering how to respond to something my children may have done that I don't like. I try to give them the love they need to get through the issue they are dealing with. (Don't mix up discipline with love.) Intuitively, they know that my actions are based on love and that the strength of my love for them is unbreakable.

So, if you have to start somewhere (before you pick up another self-help book), base your actions on love. (The good news is that you don't have to tell anyone and, again, you don't have to move to Salt Spring Island to do this.)

EXERCISE 4: Find Your Core Values

Most people have five to seven core values. To identify yours, begin by getting into the right emotional state. Clear your mind of preconceived notions and be open for new thought while you work through this exercise.

Step 1: Get in Touch with Your Values

1. Can you recall a moment when you felt totally yourself? A peak moment of life when you were in your element, when everything just felt aligned? A moment when you felt happy and fulfilled? Take some time to recall this peak moment. When you're ready, take notes describing this moment in detail. What made it important, and how did you feel?

2. Now consider a time when you were upset, angry, or frustrated. What upset you, and why? What core values were being suppressed in that moment? Write those thoughts down in a separate column.

3. Finally, in a third column, write down what is important to you. What must you have to feel fulfilled? New opportunities to learn? Travel and adventure? A strong sense of stability?

Step 2: Group and Consolidate Your Lists

Now, take your three lists and group similar words/ideas together. For instance, adventure, travel, and new experiences are values that group together, as are stability, predictability, and dependability. Then refine those groups into the words that most accurately describe each group, until each column can be succinctly described by one or two words. For example, if the Golden Rule is one of your values—"Do unto others as you would like them to do unto you"—you might sum it up as "Give love."

Step 3: Rank and Define Those Words

You should have five to ten words or phrases at this stage. The final step is to take your values and rank them according to importance, then define what each word means in the context of your life. The most effective value statements are ones that use inspiring words and trigger an emotional response. If integrity is one of your core values, for example, your value statement might be: "Integrity, to live authentically, as I believe, without apology."

Voilà! You now have a set of core values. Here are mine:

Ann's Core Values

1. Love is all there is—when in doubt, give love.
2. Be the example—be the person you want your children to be.
3. Own it—you are accountable for your actions, words, and thoughts.

4. Integrity—I am not for sale, at any price.
5. Happiness is a choice—I choose to be happy.
6. Give freely—without expectation or hesitation.

Step 4: Put Your Core Values to Work

Once you've identified your core values, use them as your guide. Review them before you make a decision. Ask yourself, how well does the outcome I expect from this decision or opportunity align with each of my values? (You may find it useful to score the decision on a scale of one through five for each value. The goal is to score an average of four or higher.) Check in with your values on a daily (or, at the very least, weekly) basis to keep you focused on what's important to you. (On the subway home from work, or driving in your car, think about your day and consider how well your actions and decisions aligned with your core values, and what you can improve upon the next day.)

Finally, remind yourself why your core values mean so much to you. Post an image of the happiness that awaits you on your fridge or phone, or make it your screen saver. Leave a visual cue to help you keep track as you work toward your bright future, and to fortify you in weak moments when you want to give up.

KNOWING THE VALUES that you live for will empower you to focus on what matters most to you—and that may be the greatest value of all.

I once gave an inspirational talk
on the importance of feeding
your brain and your body,
all while the hotel served up
pasta with cream sauce
and brownies. Everyone
left feeling full—of guilt.

#IRONY

(5)

KALE, BROCCOLI, AND WHY BURGERS ARE TRUMP'S ENEMY

---

*The food you eat can be either the safest
and most powerful form of medicine
OR the slowest form of poison.*

ANN WIGMORE

W HEN I MET my Stephen twenty years ago, he was about thirty pounds heavier than he is now. On our very first date he took me (a vegan!) to Kentucky Fried Chicken. Future dates followed with a bit more variety, ranging from Lick's Homeburgers to Golden Griddle.

I remember watching in horror while he wolfed down burgers and french fries smothered in ketchup and capped it off with a milkshake. His mainstay, I discovered, was fast food, supplemented by more fast food and, on occasion, canned food. Vegetables played a walk-on role in his diet, and Stephen refused any moderation to the comfort foods he had come to love. If it's not out of a tin, it's not *real* tomato soup, and if I put parsley on it, I was somehow deceiving him. *Real men* don't eat parsley!

In the context of Stephen, those food preferences made sense. As a former professional hockey player (he played for the Colorado Flames and Rögle BK in Sweden), he spent his youth zigzagging across the country on buses, fuelling up on takeout. I, on the other hand, grew up in a house with a large garden filled with fruit trees. I used to eat beans straight from the vine. My bouquet when we last renewed our wedding vows was made out of broccoli. I absolutely *love* vegetables (especially dark-green ones).

After the initial shock, I eventually got used to Stephen's dietary habits. Even after we married, I didn't do anything to encourage him to change his diet. I cooked his favourite foods and would make something vegan for myself on the side. The only restrictions I set were:

a) I wouldn't allow the children to go to a fast-food restaurant or to order in. (To this day, we've never done either.)

b) I refused to open a package of prepared food. Everything I cook, I cook from scratch.

Slowly, Stephen started trying different foods. I would offer him a taste of my coconut curry (he was shocked how good it could taste!) and sesame tofu (he was less enamoured of that). But it was only when faced with a health scare that he bought into the idea that the food he ate could affect his overall health.

The excuse of his strong Irish genes and the healthy family history was tossed out along with the french fries. He began to pay attention to what he was consuming, to his weight, and to his health.

After a significant change in diet, Stephen has shown an improvement in digestion, looks healthier, and has lost the thirty extra pounds he carried when I was first married to him. Stephen didn't diet to lose weight, he didn't eat less, he just started eating healthy; the thirty-pound reduction was a bonus.

(He still doesn't eat broccoli, though.)

The Second Principle

In life, there are two scenarios where you can count on someone to seek every resource available to buoy their success:

- When they are training for the Olympics
- When they've been diagnosed with a life-threatening illness

When the stakes are high—when a gold medal or your life is on the line—it becomes easy to embrace the idea of healthy eating, of fuelling your body with the types of foods that will help you achieve extraordinary goals, and of avoiding those that are counterproductive. But what about all the life scenarios in between?

We all know that good eating habits give you the best chance at a long and healthy life. Knowing that what we consume on a daily basis can keep our bodies in premium shape, knowing we are intelligent mammals with the ability to make decisions, to do research, and to decide what we put on the end of a fork, it's hard to fathom why anyone would choose to eat unhealthy foods. And yet North Americans make a habit of doing so all the time. President Trump, the leader of the free world, is renowned for his love of fast food. His typical order is reported to be two Big Macs, two Filet-O-Fish sandwiches, and a large chocolate shake![3]

Now, you might be asking yourself, "What the heck does this have to do with success?!" I'd argue *everything*—which is why nutritional intelligence (or understanding how your diet affects you) is the second principle of success. And I'm going to explain why. But first, some context.

A Growing Concern

We're fortunate in North America to have the best foods in the world at our disposal. We can easily access spices, herbs, and bananas (in a country that doesn't even grow bananas). We can have strawberries in the winter and fresh lime leaves year-round. Foods that we take for granted, such as apples and oranges, are waiting within easy reach at the corner store. And yet, more often than not, we snatch up the candy bar and a sugary beverage.

It's no secret that North America is growing—its waistline. According to the latest data from Statistics Canada, 61.8% of men (8.2 million) and 46.2% of women (6.1 million) reported height and weight that classified as obese or overweight in

---

3   washingtonpost.com/politics/trumps-campaign-big-macs-screaming-fits-and-constant-rivalries/2017/12/02/18bcfa30-d6bd-11e7-b62d-d9345ced896d_story.html?noredirect=ON&utm_term=.3779afa982d7

2014. Those numbers have been rising since 2003,[4] and dramatically so in the most at-risk group. An astounding 20.2% of Canadians classified as obese in 2014, representing a 27% and 22% rise in obesity in men and women, respectively, in just over a decade.

In the USA, the numbers are even more dire. According to a 2017 report by the National Center for Health Statistics, nearly 40% of American adults are obese, an increase of 30% since 1999,[5] and a further 32.8% are overweight.[6] That means the vast majority—70.7% of American adults—struggle to manage their weight.

In short, we're getting fatter—and fast!

This is not breaking news. The obesity epidemic in North America is a complex and multi-faceted issue that has been written about ad nauseam in magazines, newspapers, books, and white papers. It's even prompted a fat pride countermovement. Well-founded concerns over rising rates of weight-associated diseases such as diabetes, high blood pressure, and heart disease and stroke, the number one cause of premature death in the USA,[7] are refuted with "Love your curves!" messaging. Yes, we should love our curves, and size does not matter—but health does. We're eating ourselves to an early grave by ignoring that.

---

4   statcan.gc.ca/pub/82-625-x/2015001/article/14185-eng.htm

5   cdc.gov/nchs/products/databriefs/db288.htm

6   cdc.gov/nchs/fastats/obesity-overweight.htm

7   cdc.gov/nchs/fastats/leading-causes-of-death.htm

Food for Success

We know that the way we eat is hurting us, as a society. What if we understood food and exercise not just as vital to our personal well-being but as tools for living a successful life? What if we regarded physical health as one of the fundamental principles of success?

I fervently believe that health is one of the most overlooked factors in modern success. Let me repeat that: **health is one of the most overlooked factors in modern success.** If you are not of a healthy mind and body, you cannot expect to function at your best. Nor will you *feel* at your best. You can have all the trappings of success—good job, high income, fancy car—but without your health you will not be able to enjoy any of it. In the axiom "health, wealth, and happiness," health comes first.

So let's start with the food fuelling your success (or lack thereof).

The Pleasure Argument . . . How Did We Get Here?

While the causes of obesity are numerous, researchers believe that the single largest contributing factor is excess caloric intake.[8] Simply put, we eat too much. One "heavyweight" in this battle is our over reliance on fast and convenience foods (*cough* the Stephen diet). Before we had the ability to pull up to a window 24/7 and order 2,000 calories in a single sitting,

---

8 nejm.org/doi/full/10.1056/NEJMhpro905723

people cooked—actual food. Often from scratch! In those days of old, adult obesity rates were much lower (approximately 10%), people walked, and baby oil was accepted sun care. (Okay, so it wasn't *all* perfect.)

Today, the food industry is run by marketers, offering conveniently prepackaged sugar with little thought behind the nutritional value. Wrapped in buns and fried into bite-sized portions, they make consumption simple. "Deliciously simple," some would say. *Dangerously* simple might be more accurate.

We've allowed ourselves to be programmed to satisfy the pleasure centre in our brains, to chase the fleeting thrill of a sugar high. And this is changing not just the way we eat but the way we think. Neuroscientists have shown that sugar leads to the release of the mood-regulating neurotransmitter dopamine in the nucleus accumbens, an area of the brain associated with novelty, motivation, and reward. It's the same part of the brain that responds to cocaine and heroin. And we become addicted to it. Like street drugs, binge-eating foods high in sugar or fat can cause neurochemical changes in the brain that keep us wanting more.

Add sleep deprivation and chronic stress to the mix and you create a perfect storm of poor eating choices. Studies show that high levels of anxiety and lack of sleep diminish willpower, making us more susceptible to seeking out foods high in fat and sugar for the positive effects they create on the reward centre of the brain. Never mind that this stuff bloats you, stuffs you, or shows up in protest on your forehead or cheeks.

In the rush to "fast is good, cheap is better" food, we have lost the idea of fuelling our bodies with food that is nourishing. It's not that healthy food is inconvenient or even expensive; fresh produce is typically one of the lowest-ticket items on a grocery list. It's that we've been programmed to reach for the prepackaged item of the day, and then we develop a craving for that food. In essence, it is not the food that could get spoiled, it is us. North America has a very messed-up view of food, and we eat right into it.

Good Food Is the Answer

But food can also be the solution. It can be the cure that restores, rejuvenates, and rewards your body. Numerous studies indicate that a diet of whole foods rich in antioxidants, vitamins, and healthy fats will aid in recovery, assist in the rejuvenation of healthy cells, and prevent disease, including cancer, heart disease, and diabetes. When we're ill, we can even change the course of our disease with what we eat. A diet rich in fruits and vegetables can put the fight in us, giving us the energy and nutritional firepower we need to fuel our recovery!

The question is, then, why wait until our health is impaired before we fix it? Why must fear be our guide? We hear stories of people diagnosed with type 2 diabetes and heart disease who made radical changes in their diet and took control of their health when the odds were stacked against them. The same goes for weight gain. Why must we have to deal with negative aspects of excess weight before we consider a diet that will help us stay mentally balanced, energetic, and at a healthy weight, primed for success?

You don't have to wait until you are faced with an impending crisis to adopt a healthy diet.

Faulty Logic

We all know that healthy eating will make us feel and look better. But, like folding the laundry and paying parking tickets, we come up with reasons (read: excuses) either to procrastinate or to rationalize the poor shape we are in. We say things like:

- People should accept me as I am.
- I can work off the extra calories at the gym.
- I had a bad day, I deserve this doughnut/drink/family-size bag of Doritos.
- "Desserts" is "stressed" spelled backwards.
- Hasn't hurt me so far!
- This is just how middle age *looks*.
- I "thought" about working out today. That counts, right?
- Everyone in my family/friend group is overweight.
- [Insert your excuse here.]

We justify our failure to focus on creating healthier habits, and when we do choose somewhat healthy foods, we tend to consume them in larger portions or add a heaping side of calories. I'm talking about that twenty-four-ounce steak topped with bacon and served with a side of fries, dessert, and an alcoholic drink—*or three*. We rationalize by insisting that one choice discounts the other.

Or we justify eating unhealthy foods by slightly reducing the amount of it we eat or by the hint of a healthy ingredient. It's Number 45 ordering a burger with a half bun "in service of his health."[9] It's thinking that if the label says, "kale added,"

9 independent.co.uk/life-style/food-and-drink/donald-trump-burger-order-half-bun-rudy-giuliani-us-president-a8352376.html

"ANTIOXIDANT," or "gluten free!" then it must be good for you, right?

Wrong.

Eat with Purpose

Adopting a healthier diet doesn't have to be an overwhelming task. You don't have to start growing and canning your own tomatoes or making homemade pesto from your organic herb garden. It can be as simple as driving by the drive-thru. Start small. Aim to look up a recipe or two on the Internet, to make more regular trips to the produce section. I, personally, eat based on two principles: the food I consume has to "work for me in some way" and it cannot "work against me."

First Rule of Healthy Eating: Make Good Choices

Okay, if you're on the Stephen diet or are prone to 4 a.m. trips to the refrigerator, there are a few things you will have to change. Finding foods that satisfy you and are actually good for you will take some investigation. I am guessing that you already know deep-fried food, sugar-laden sweets, and ice cream in the wee morning hours may not be the best choice. But it is possible to find foods that taste great and are good for you. It doesn't have to taste like Styrofoam or feel like you're chewing on drywall chips to be healthy.

Nor does eating healthy require an onerous amount of reconnaissance work. These foods are not hidden away in a small-town farmers' market or on the overpriced shelves of Whole Foods. You don't need a grocery Sherpa to track one down. They're everywhere! In fact, they have been in front

of us most of our lives—hidden in the pasta, sprinkled on a pizza, or (if we were so unlucky growing up) overcooked and mixed into our mashed potatoes. It's not a matter of finding these foods, it's a simple question of opening our fridge doors to them.

Take broccoli. Broccoli is a perfect example of a wildly underappreciated vegetable that has not been given its due. Broccoli is not a side dish to be ignored, an afterthought in your meal planning, destined to wilt in your icebox. It's a bona fide champion among vegetables. The Clark Kent of produce! Beneath its unassuming green crowns, a nutritional super-hero abides:

1. Broccoli is loaded with cancer-fighting antioxidants and fibre.
2. Broccoli is a rich source of vitamin C to aid in iron absorption.

3. It is also high in calcium to help control blood pressure and build strong bones.
4. Broccoli is shown to aid in digestion, prevent chronic diseases, and boost both brain health and your immune system.
5. Broccoli alkalizes the body.
6. Broccoli is a good source of protein.
7. Consuming large quantities of broccoli will not contribute to weight gain.
8. Broccoli can even improve sexual performance.
9. And it combats aging!

In short, broccoli does everything short of your taxes! It is your body's best friend.

If there's a problem with this superfood, it's the way people prepare it. Overcooking broccoli, adding too much salt, or smothering it in cheese sauce are all proven ways to disguise the inner beauty of broccoli, a food that needs little more than a bit of seasoning and garlic (another antioxidant) to taste great.

(Comedian Ellen DeGeneres, a fellow vegan, shares similar feelings about the Cruciferae. She devoted an entire chapter in her hilarious memoir *Seriously... I'm Kidding* to "that which will save the world." That chapter had one word in it: "Kale." Personally, I prefer spinach. But I digress.)

The point is broccoli (and its leafy green friends) deserve a chance on your dinner plate.

Second Rule of Healthy Eating: Avoid Foods That Are Bad for You

Your food should work for you, not against you. What you eat shouldn't be something you need to work off in the gym or that spends the next few days clogging your arteries. Success, in the long term, is not fuelled by a deep-dish, cheese-stuffed-crust pizza. And no, topping it with a bit of green pepper does not make up for the rest. Not even broccoli can do that.

Nutrition is not a negotiation, like discussing mortgage rates or where you might take your spouse for dinner. Also, you should never negotiate with yourself. Make it a rule to avoid foods that are unhealthy. You may enjoy those foods, you may indulge in them on occasion and in moderation (and eventually not at all). But let them be the exception, not the rule.

For me, a typical day includes fresh (antioxidant-rich) berries, pomegranates, and roasted nuts in the morning, a vegetable and chickpea curry for lunch, and, usually, more Asian-inspired vegetables for dinner. (Disclaimer: I eat a lot of Thai curry. But rarely with rice.) The exceptions to my good-choices rule are instant coffee and cheap Chardonnay. (Nobody is perfect.)

Third Rule of Healthy Eating:
Set Yourself Up for Success

It's not enough to wish for changes in our eating habits—we have to plan for them. Consciously. Intentionally. And sometimes with strict adherence to the healthy eating practices (also known as trying to lose weight after forty). The simplest way to live a healthy life is to surround yourself with healthy choices, and that starts with what's in your kitchen (and tucked away in the nightstand).

Think of five to ten things you can do immediately, right this minute, to set yourself up so that healthy options are your default choice. Here—I started the list for you:

- Get rid of foods in your home that are not healthy...
- ...including in the bottom cupboard and your nightstand drawer.
- Fill the cookie jar with almonds. (But not chocolate-covered almonds.)

- Stock up on foods that do a body good—spinach, berries, nuts.
- Avoid foods that you have to counter with two hours in the gym and/or that give you instant food regret.
- Keep healthy snacks within arm's reach.
- Have a bowl of fresh fruit out at all times.
- Drink two glasses of water thirty minutes before each meal.
- Eat until you are slightly full, not feeling heavy.
- Remind yourself that vegetables are delicious!

Food Is Just One Part of the Equation

We started this chapter talking about health and how looking after yours is the second principle in living a successful life. What you put into your body is only one factor in that equation, however. Being body aware is also about being physically strong. It is about being mobile, it is about touching your toes and stretching, about proactively and continuously being in shape. We'll talk more about that in the next chapter.

The take-away message here is that you need to pay attention to what you're putting into your body. When you think of food as the fuel of your success, you'll be empowered to make better choices, and you will look and feel better as a result. If you're like Stephen, you may even lose a few pounds in the process. (But dropping half a bun from your burger won't do it.)

EXERCISE 5: The Food Experiment

The saying "you are what you eat" describes more than how you look; it is reflected in the physical makeup of who you are. Every twenty-seven days, your skin replaces itself. Your liver, every 150 to 500 days. Your bones, every ten years. White blood cells regenerate every year. Your body makes these cells from the foods you consume, so it follows that you should want to build yourself out of the best possible materials.

Set yourself up to make good choices, develop healthy eating habits, and introduce new body-boosting helpers into your diet.

1. **Try again (and again):** If you have not tried a food, you may not have acquired a taste for it. Generally, we learn our taste preferences during our formative years when we are exposed to the foods of our family and culture. You can *learn* to like a food, however. Even broccoli. A 2010 study[10] found that children who tried a vegetable they previously didn't like at least eight or nine times began to like it more. Think of it like Stockholm syndrome for your taste buds.

2. **Prepare foods differently:** There is a significant difference between Brussels sprouts boiled to a dull grey mush and Brussels sprouts sprinkled with olive oil, garlic, salt, pepper, and balsamic vinegar and roasted to a crisp in the oven. Kale does not have to be bitter; younger kale generally tastes better julienned thin, and rubbed with lemon, olive oil, salt, and pepper. Even tofu can taste great when prepared properly! (Pinky swear.)

   When in doubt, experiment with a different preparation method. Try flash-frying or adding spices and herbs from different cultures to enhance flavours in adventurous ways.

3. **Commit to pure food:** If you consider the food you consume as an energy source, an anti-inflammatory agent, a cancer preventer, or a catalyst for great skin, you will be more cognizant

---

10 ncbi.nlm.nih.gov/pubmed/20541572

of what you put in your body. Your diet is a powerful predictor of your health.

4. **Skip the processed-food aisles:** Do away with cans and packages. Learn to cook the basics, date someone who cooks the basics, hire someone to cook the basics! Whatever it takes, figure out easy ways to introduce healthy foods into your diet. Eating healthy should not take over your life; it should be a way of life. (That includes broccoli. Seriously. It's delicious.)

5. **Look for healthier options:** Restaurants are full of healthy choices. Gluten-free options are on almost every menu and (pro tip!) you can choose to drive by the Tim Hortons. Dine at establishments that offer fresh food options.

They say beauty is
in the eye of the beholder.
Turns out,
I'm the beholder.

(6)

YOUR BODY IS A TEMPLE

If you always put a limit on everything you do, physical or anything else, it will spread into your work and into your life. There are no limits, there are only plateaus, and you must not stay there, you must go beyond them.

BRUCE LEE

WHEN I WAS in my early twenties, I made a brief foray into the world of professional bodybuilding. Every day after work, I'd ride my bike to Gold's Gym on Blanshard Street in Victoria, BC, and work out. *In sweatpants.* At the time, I didn't really know what bodybuilding was or even realize I was buff until the owner of the gym asked me if I wanted to compete.

Naturally, I said yes. (Seize opportunities!) And then immediately became obsessed with getting as fit as humanly possible.

(Type A personality!) If I was going to a friend's house, I'd ride my bike, in the lowest gear, with weights on my ankles. If I was sodium-depleting before a competition (as was the conventional wisdom at the time), I'd research how much sodium was in everything I consumed, including tap water. *And saliva.* Then ponder spitting both out.

I used every moment of every day to be in the ultimate shape. And it paid off. I came second in both the individual and couples divisions at BC Nationals, I did an opening for TSN Sports Network, flexing onstage to Queen's "Body Language," and I spent a season as the national poster girl for Gold's Gym.

Then I decided I like drinking water and so concluded my bodybuilding career.

The Third Principle

You don't have to be cut like 1980 Arnold Schwarzenegger to be successful in life. You should, at a minimum, be able to take a flight of stairs without getting winded, easily bend over to tie your shoes, and not think twice about going for a walk on a sunny day. You know, *live.*

Being fit for success is about more than the convenience of moving with ease, it's about developing a high body intelligence (or BQ), the third principle of success. How you take care of your body has a direct impact on your work, your health, and your happiness. Your physical fitness affects your self-confidence and state of mind. It determines your energy levels and weight. It even impacts how your brain functions. According to neuroscientist Wendy Suzuki, exercise is the most transformative thing you can do for your brain; a single work-out will immediately increase levels of neurotransmitters such as dopamine, serotonin, and noradrenalin.[11]

Successful people know this. According to Tom Corley, author of *Change Your Habits, Change Your Life*, 76% of rich people do aerobic exercise for thirty minutes or more every day. Clif Bar CEO Kevin Cleary is so invested in the health benefits of exercise, he pays his employees for working out at least two and a half hours a week.

For the majority of North Americans, however, fitness, like diet, is often an overlooked tool in building success, which is ironic, because we don't have to look far to see the impact of *not* looking after our physical well-being. If you spend your mornings recovering from the night before, if your mind is cloudy, if you are overly tired, are feeling bloated, and/or lose your breath at the slightest exertion, you're not fit to function at your best—in any arena. Just as an athlete would be ill-advised to indulge in an evening of tequila shots at the pub the night before a big game, you cannot expect to per-form at your optimum when you're not taking optimal care of your body.

Now, here's where it gets tricky. It is not about the "night before the game." It's about training yourself to nurture healthy habits. It is about living a life where you are positively con-tributing to your physical well-being and making choices that support your success. There's no multivitamin that will give you a clear mind, optimal energy, or a fit body. You'll have to work at being in physical shape. *Or not.*

---

11 ted.com/talks/wendy_suzuki_the_brain_changing_benefits_of_exercise?language=en

Ten Proven Ways to Stay out of Shape

Much has been written on how to get in shape. There's *The Couch Potato's Guide to Getting Fit,* the aerobics classic *Sweatin' to the Oldies,* and endless iterations of CrossFit and yoga. You probably already have a good idea which athletic endeavours you're willing to try and which ones you have zero interest in. Here are a few ways to successfully *not* get in shape, inspired by the 70% of North Americans who don't get the recommended weekly amount of aerobic and muscle-building exercise.

1. Watch other people work out (while snacking on a McDonald's combo).
2. Be a hard-core sports fan (but don't ever play).
3. Take the elevator (even if it's only up one floor).
4. Start a fad diet (the Bacon Diet! Fruitarianism! Paleo!).
5. Stock your pantry with junk food but promise yourself you'll only eat it on "cheat day."
6. Sign up for the "cool" gym across town.
7. Compare yourself to others (and feel your self-love grow).
8. Find a workout you hate.
9. Seek moral support from people who enjoy putting you down.
10. Listen to sad, sad songs.

Not helpful? The fact is, we self-sabotage all the time. If you find yourself saying "I used to ski" or "In high school, I ran track and field" or "I was never athletic," you're subtly setting yourself up to fail before you even begin.

Here are some other common ways we get in your own way when it comes to fitness.

"I'm Too Old."

If you were once a star athlete and now have a soft centre, getting into peak physical condition is going to seem daunting. So don't. Aim to get into *better* shape. Numerous studies have shown that even relatively minor amounts of exercise will transform your life in spectacular ways, boosting your memory, concentration, and cognitive abilities, as well as your libido.

You don't have to commit to training for the next Olympics (although why not?) or to the gruelling regime of a competitive athlete. Getting fit is about taking control of your well-being and empowering yourself to look and feel your best. Great-grandmother Flo Meiler took up track and field at the ripe young age of sixty and, in the twenty-odd years since, has earned twenty-five world records and more than 750 medals. (She competes in the triple jump, hammer throw, discus, shot put, hurdles, 50-metre run, 100-metre run, 200-metre run, and pole vaulting!) Long-distance swimmer Diana Nyad became the first person to swim from Florida to Cuba without a protective shark cage—at sixty-four years of age! My sister started tai chi at age forty-five and now she can almost touch her toes!

It's never too late to work on improving your fitness.

"I Don't Have Time."

Life is busy! Fitting daily exercise into your already packed schedule can seem like an impossible feat. You may think things like, *I don't have time to work out. I can barely fit in laundry, let alone going to the gym.* I get it. Some days I run about the office like a headless chicken, signing cheques, taking calls, juggling meetings, all while filtering through 700-plus e-mails, and that's before lunch. But here's a hard truth: we *do* have time to exercise and also cook healthy foods and get enough sleep every day. We just don't *make those things a priority.*

Every week, we have 168 hours to spend. That time is our most precious resource and we allocate it to the things we deem most important. It's just that sometimes we're prioritizing the wrong things. (See: smartphones.) If you fall down a Facebook hole before bed every night, have weekly Netflix-and-chill marathons, or even just watch a show every day, you have time to fit in a brisk twenty-minute walk.

The trick is to become aware of where exactly you're spending your minutes and to decide if those tasks are contributing to your happiness or wasting it. And, hey, if you just can't give up your nightly episode of *Grey's Anatomy*, try doing crunches at the same time. There is *always* a way to fit in a bit of fitness.

"But I Can't Afford a Gym Membership."

Did I say anything about gym? No one said you have to spend money to be in shape. Personally, it always strikes me as odd that people pay to run on a treadmill. I remember being in a hotel in Vancouver, arguably one of the most beautiful and clean cities in the world, and watching rows and rows of sweaty people pumping away on treadmills overlooking the ocean when they could have been running along a spectacular seawall right outside the door!

Sure, if going to a gym gets you motivated, you should do that. But you don't have to pay to bend your knees and touch your toes. Walking and running are free. There's no fee for squats. You don't even have to buy an at-home workout video—there are millions of free ones on YouTube! Do whatever keeps you active, and commit to doing it on a regular basis.

"I'll Get Fit in the New Year."

"I'll get fit for my fiftieth birthday." "I'll get back to the gym when work slows down/when the kids are a bit older." "After I lose a few pounds, I'll get into a regular workout schedule." Getting in shape can seem like this formidable task that future-you will magically find the time for—*when life is less demanding.*

I'll let you in on a little secret: there *is* a perfect time to start working on your fitness that is proven to yield the best results. It's right now. Today! This minute, even! So go on, head out for a walk already. I'll wait . . .

"But It Hurts."

In the beginning, increasing your activity level is probably going to reward you with a few sore muscles. But it's temporary and it gets easier. Eventually, working out is going to feel incredible! Take it from a former bodybuilder.

Things That Inevitably Happen When You Start to Get in Shape

Once you start getting more fit, a number of wonderful things will start to manifest in your life:

1. **Your mind will be sharper.** Exercise boosts blood flow to the brain, enabling your brain cells to function at a higher level. You'll be cleverer, more clear-headed, and less likely to misplace your keys. Research shows that working out may even help you think more creatively.[12] It's also shown to help prevent

---

12 bigthink.com/videos/wendy-suzuki-on-can-exercise-enhance-creativity

dementia, so you'll have a lower risk of losing your mind later on in life. (It will not prevent your partner from driving you insane, though. There's no workout regime for that.)

2. **You'll feel more self-confident.** Getting in shape does wonders for your body image. You'll stop worrying about the number on the scale (muscle weighs more than fat, after all) because you'll be so enamoured of how great you feel! You'll carry yourself more confidently and have better posture. You'll have better sex too!

3. **You'll be happier.** Exercise releases endorphins and other feel-good brain chemicals that promote happiness. According to researchers at the University of Vermont, just twenty minutes of exercise can produce mood-boosting effects that last twelve hours. Those mood-boosting effects are even greater when we exercise outside.

4. **You'll experience less stress.** Exercise reduces levels of the stress hormones cortisol and adrenalin in the body, which means working out helps alleviate worry. In fact, it's a proven remedy for depression and anxiety.

5. **Your skin will glow.** Research shows that exercise not only helps to keep skin younger, it may even reverse skin aging in people who start exercising later in life.

6. **Your social life will improve.** Exercising makes you popular! *Just kidding.* The improvement in your self-esteem and happiness may improve your social relations, though. You'll be more likely to reach out to others and forge new friendships with people who share your interests. It's also an excellent way to connect with your existing friends. I remember the times

I spend walking, fishing, skiing, or paddle-boarding with my friends and children more than times we share over a meal or a coffee.

7. **Nothing will hold you back.** One of the greatest rewards of living a proactively fit lifestyle is that you will not, later in life, have to fix the damage you caused by living an unhealthy life. You will not have to lose weight or start going to the gym, because you will already be fit. There is no big training day to run that race, because you've already trained. There is also nothing holding you back from the life you dream of.

. . . .

The ultimate goal of a blessed life is physical health and mental serenity.

EPICURUS

. . . .

Now Take a Nap

No, really. Getting enough rest plays a vital role in our well-being. Personally, it's probably the thing I'm worst at prioritizing, but there is no shortage of reasons we should all be striving for a good night's rest. Inadequate sleep is strongly linked to weight gain and obesity. It negatively affects cognition, concentration, productivity, and performance. It's even linked to risk of heart disease and stroke, type 2 diabetes, and depression. Good sleep counters all of those things and is shown to enhance athletic performance, improve immune function, and boost mood, to boot. So don't skip out on the zzz's!

Listen to Your Body Talk

We've established that your body, and how you care for it, plays a starring role in your success, directly impacting your thoughts, feelings, self-confidence, and energy levels. We also know that your body is constantly telling you things. Like a trusted confidant, it's privy to your most intimate aches, pains, and physical shortcomings. The question is: are you listening? Or are you pressing Ignore Call when your body pipes up?

Too often we pay no heed to the messages our body is sending us, opting for caffeine over rest, wine over workouts. Make it a point to check in with your body every day. Are you breaking a sweat on a regular basis? Do you wake up feeling rested? How does the food you eat make you feel? Having a high BQ means eating well, regular exercise, and adequate rest—it means setting yourself up for success. And occasionally it means sporting a string bikini and a fake tan to flex your biceps onstage.

EXERCISE 6: Boost Your BQ

Pop quiz! Being physically fit means doing things that contribute toward your fitness—on a regular basis. The goal is to do some type of exercise every day, ideally for a minimum of twenty to thirty minutes without stopping. Sometimes it's as simple as booking "walking meetings" at work (long walks were Steve Jobs's preferred way to conduct a serious conversation), biking to the office, or roughhousing with your kids. Make a list of ten things you can do immediately to work toward a fitter you.

I'm not actually funny.
I am really smart.
I tell it like it is and people
think I'm hysterical . . .
Now *that's* funny.

(7)

SMART IS THE NEW SEXY

**The greatest enemy of
knowledge is not ignorance, it is
the illusion of knowledge.**

STEPHEN HAWKING

LOVE A GOOD brain. I absolutely crave a knowledgeable person at the table—almost as much as broccoli. Great humour (definitely a sign of intelligence), a learned thinker, an inquisitive mind, a person with an opinion who, regardless how they deliver it, has something smart to contribute—those are incredibly attractive features. Sexiest man ever? Stephen Hawking, hands down.

But while I have a deep appreciation of intelligence, I don't always *feel* smart.

When I was doing my MBA, I felt downright inefficient, inept, inadequate, as though I lacked what it took to pursue a business degree. I worried that someone would discover I was not as knowledgeable as my classmates, that not only did I struggle to learn how to calculate a beta, I didn't even really know what it was! I thought I had to work harder than they did just to get through (which was, in itself, embarrassing. Why did some people find it so easy?). I slogged. I toiled at it. I took extra courses and sought help—all the while not realizing that I was learning to learn, that I was stretching and strengthening my worn brain.

And, as hard as it was, it began to feel good. The more I worked, the more I reaped the benefits of a good mental workout. I was training a muscle, and it got progressively stronger and more flexible. I felt a yearning to learn more and try to put pieces together. Everything I learned ended with another question to try to answer, another "Why?" I completed my MBA empowered with the knowledge that (if I put the effort in) I could do it.

I went on to do a master's in science, a corporate governance designation (ICD.D), and then a doctorate. And it only became more difficult each time. When I reached the PhD level, I felt completely inadequate all over again. The process of learning to learn had been swept under the rug when the task of synthesizing that knowledge took over. I had to apply research to theory. I had to take what I learned, find answers for what I didn't know, and develop my own theory about it all. I had to rethink how I thought about, well, thought!

Then a light went on. I had spent so much time working at the art of "knowledge building," at reading, learning, studying, and synthesizing what I had learned, that I had shaped my brain into a different way of thinking. Everything started to make sense and I felt empowered again, knowing that there is no absolute answer to my queries. I learned that limitations are okay, that citing your sources helps establish credibility, and that, when all else fails, just say you're a doctor and people will assume you're smart. (Kidding![13])

My point is, it can be tremendously hard work to acquire new information. Sometimes the task is downright daunting, and the Herculean effort required to learn something new may feel as if it's splitting your brain in two. But if you keep at it, if you struggle through it, you'll find the fruits of that labour are ever so sweet.

The Fourth Principle

For me, academia is a second home. But degrees and higher education are just one path to knowledge. (Please don't tell my kids I said that.) There's no shortage of fiercely intelligent and accomplished college dropouts—Bill Gates, Steve Jobs, Frank Lloyd Wright, James Cameron, and Mark Zuckerberg, to name a few. And still others who didn't even finish high school (Walt Disney, Charles Dickens, Richard Branson, and Quentin Tarantino among them). You don't need a formal education to be a student of life. You do need an unwavering love of learning.

Buddhists call this "beginner's mind" or "*Shoshin.*" The idea is to approach a subject, even one you know well, with an attitude of openness, eagerness, and lack of preconceptions, just as a beginner would. Successful people inherently embody

---

13 From my lawyer: "Impersonating a doctor is a criminal offence, Ann. Please strike from the book."

a beginner's mind. They make learning new ideas, exploring different concepts, and expanding their world view a priority in their daily lives, no matter how full their schedule may already be. Microsoft magnate Bill Gates (who these days is busy saving the world via the Bill & Melinda Gates Foundation) publishes his reading list online every month, and it isn't just a list of book titles. He writes entire blog posts articulating what he likes about a book and how it applies to his understanding of the world.

It's no coincidence that people who strive for personal growth are also those who tend to thrive in their professional lives. Knowledge is as necessary to a successful life as water, love, and rosemary-roasted nuts. Without feeding our brains, asking questions, reading great self-help books (*ahem*), we do not give ourselves the opportunity to build and deepen our understanding of the world.

Investing in knowledge, ultimately, is investing in success— and that's why the pursuit of knowledge is the fourth principle of success.

....

Who you are or what you are means nothing. Handicaps mean even less. Most of our richest men started as poor boys. Many of our best educated men spent very little time in high school, let alone college. Our great inventors have no formal scientific training. The world's greatest heroes—look at Napoleon, Pasteur, Lindberg—have always been surprises—dark horses.

DARTNELL CORPORATION

....

Can Intelligence Be Learned?

Before I first gave birth, I wondered the same thing: Can intelligence be learned? Does the way I bring up my child contribute to how intelligent they will become, or did their father dilute the gene pool[14] so much that the kid has no hope?

I spent time researching this very topic and stumbled upon the Better Baby Institute in Philadelphia (now called The Institutes for the Achievement of Human Potential). Founded by Glenn Doman, the institute is internationally known for its work with brain-damaged children. Doman felt that a child with a developmental or learning disability could realize their full potential with appropriate sensory stimulation if taught at a very young age, and, what's more, that neurotypical children could achieve excellence using the same strategies.

I attended his workshop before I had my first child and again when I had my second. What stuck with me most is "stupid in, stupid out" and, conversely, "smart in, smart out"— that intelligence can be nurtured (or stifled), and we can all, regardless of the limitations in our path, improve our cognitive abilities with effort. And you don't have to be a child for it to be effective. Current research on neuroplasticity in the aging brain shows that cognitive training is surprisingly durable over time.[15] If you are willing and have a pulse, you have the ability to become more intelligent. (Aren't you glad you bought this book? Next one comes with a highlighter.)

---

14 If the only two things I ever do to my ex-husband are dedicate my book *Best Practices: Managing and Marketing Your Cosmetic Medical Practice in Turbulent Times* to him (because he left me a single mother with no support) and mention him in this statement, then I can affirm that the years of struggle were entirely worth it. I win.

15 ncbi.nlm.nih.gov/pmc/articles/PMC3622463/

You Can Teach an Old Dog

* *

**Imagination is more important
than knowledge. Knowledge is limited.
Imagination encircles the world.**

ALBERT EINSTEIN

* *

There is another reason to tell our children to get their education while they are young: statistically, we are unlikely to go back to university or start a formal education program after age thirty. We run out of capacity, or we just get in our own way.

But it isn't that we run out of *mental* capacity as we get older. While it's true that many older students have more difficulty learning and retaining material, they've also been found to be unusually dedicated to studying. (Phew! It's not just me.) The challenge is to get our heads around the idea of going back to school or even learning new things in the first place. We convince ourselves that we can't do something, that we don't have the ability to acquire new skills and ideas. We tell our children that they can achieve anything they set their minds to, but reach a certain age and we stop believing that about ourselves. Why is that?

It takes the same amount of energy to picture success as it does to imagine failure. Just think how much closer we'd be to achieving our goals if we harnessed all of the energy and creativity it takes to suppress our imaginations, to hold us back from achieving great things, and put even half of it toward trying! If you're creative enough to think up reasons *not* to do something you dream about, you've already demonstrated that you are creative enough to find reasons you should—and how. You just have to get out of your own way.

Knowledge Is Power

> **If knowledge can create problems, it is not through ignorance that we can solve them.**
>
> ISAAC ASIMOV

Whether they learned from books or from experience, we are inspired by individuals who use their knowledge to create solutions, build successful businesses, and change the way we think about the human condition. Elon Musk is a prime example. Musk built four multi-billion-dollar companies—in four different fields (software, aerospace, energy, and transportation)—by his mid-forties. At the foundation of his phenomenal success is a voracious and wide-ranging appetite for learning. (According to his brother, Kimbal, teenaged Musk read two books *per day* on countless subjects.) He studies widely in a diverse number of fields, gains an understanding of the underlying principles that connect those fields, and then applies that understanding to his core interest (or, in his case, core *areas* of interest) to come up with novel solutions.

"I think most people can learn a lot more than they think they can. They sell themselves short without trying," wrote Musk in a Reddit AMA. "One bit of advice: it is important to view knowledge as sort of a semantic tree—make sure you understand the fundamental principles, i.e., the trunk and big branches, before you get into the leaves/details or there is nothing for them to hang onto." You could say that investing in knowledge has paid dividends in Musk's success. It can in yours too. (And you don't have to become a super-genius speed-reader to see results!)

Knowledge Alone Is Not Enough

So, is that it? We become fit, healthy-eating individuals working on our spiritual self and sharing our feverishly clever thoughts with the world? Nope! (We're only halfway through the book...). Just because you are intelligent doesn't mean you're likeable, socially acceptable, or, for that matter, a good conversationalist. It just means you're smart.

Just as important to your success as your IQ is your EQ, or emotional intelligence—that is your ability to identify, recognize, and manage emotions in yourself and in others. EQ is so important, in fact, it's considered a predictor of success. Developing yours will be the key to managing and developing positive relationships in your life, an idea we'll explore in the next chapter.

The message to take home here is to adopt a growth mindset. Live a life where you are investing in your intellect, where you are exercising your brain. Trade movies for crossword puzzles. Read newspapers—*plural*. (Don't rely on only one news source.) Be up on current events. Watch documentaries. Be engaged. Investing in knowledge is not an exercise: it is a lifestyle. It means opening your mind to learn, to engage, and to grow—even if sometimes you have to break your brain a little to get there.

EXERCISE 7: Invest in Knowledge

There are endless ways to invest in your intellect. At every moment, you have the opportunity to be growing, developing, and learning; to be consciously building your knowledge; to pursue and provoke understanding.

1. **Be curious.** Children are curious about everything. They want to know what something tastes and feels like, why the sky is blue and the wind howls. Their sponge-like minds are ready to absorb new information at every turn. As adults, we often lose that innate curiosity. We stop asking questions about the world around us or, worse, turn a blind eye to new information and ideas before us.

    Make it a priority to seek knowledge, conscientiously and unrelentingly. Be inquisitive. Look to know more and to search out truths. Dedicate ten minutes every day to exploring something that has piqued your interest. Open your mind to new ideas, especially those that compete with your current understanding of the world.

2. **Observe.** Observation opens your mind to subtle social cues and helps you to better understand the people around you. When you're speaking with someone, observe their body language so you not only listen to what is being said but also deduce what is not being said. Train yourself to pay attention and *see* how someone feels. Your friend may tell you she's "fine," but if her eyes are red and puffy or her nails are bitten

to the quick, you can intuit that something more is going on. Listening to and understanding the feelings of others is the epicentre of empathy.

3. **Ask questions.** "Why?" The one word almost guaranteed to lead to another question. A curious mind—a mind that finds no limitations, a mind that wants to know everything that could possibly affect an outcome—is one that will never stop asking questions, because there will always be more to learn! And yet, at times, we hold back from posing questions. Isn't a question an admission of what we don't know? If we put our ego aside, we know that questions help put a conversation into perspective. By saying "I don't understand" or "How did you come to that conclusion?" you demonstrate that you are engaged with the speaker and you give yourself the opportunity to learn, to gain a better understanding of someone or something. The kicker: if you are nurturing your spiritual self, you're going to be okay with being wrong—you'll probably even laugh about it.

4. **Seek out knowledgeable people.** I don't feel that sharing knowledge is necessarily the best way to grow. How can we learn if we spend all our time talking? I like—no, I love!—to hear what other people have to say when they are sharing something new and interesting. I enjoy them more when they know their subject. (That works the other way too: I have little tolerance for strong opinions presented by someone who only reads the headlines.) I surround myself with knowledgeable people and, as a result, am inspired and enriched by their wisdom.

5. **Read more.** American self-help author Napoleon Hill said, "The way of success is the way of continuous pursuit of knowledge." British Nobel laureate Bertrand Russell wrote, "The

good life is one inspired by love but guided by knowledge." Many philosophers, business people, and great thinkers have theories on what it takes to realize success, and none of them say, "Read less."

Make reading a daily habit. Americans spend an estimated 23.6 hours *every week* texting and on social media;[16] how about we allocate some of that time to more mentally stimulating activities? If you can find the time to tweet or post on Instagram, you can carve out fifteen minutes a day to read an article, listen to a podcast, or watch a short documentary. With the World Wide Web at your fingertips, it's never been easier.

---

16 technologyreview.com/the-download/610045/the-average-american-spends-24-hours-a-week-online/

He said I drove him
to other women,
but he's wrong.
I would've paid them
to pick him up.

(8)

MARRY WELL ... REALLY, REALLY WELL (AND OTHER RELATIONSHIP ADVICE)

Give the gift of your absence to those who do not appreciate your presence.

UNKNOWN

THERE IS ALWAYS a breaking point when a marriage ends. For me, that moment came when I found out my husband had a mistress named Carol. Carol lived in Phoenix, where my husband did business development. I guess you could say he did Carol *and* business in Phoenix. Either way, he probably had little downtime.

When I found out about said Carol, I didn't confront my husband. It was just before Christmas, the time of year when you contemplate what your spouse might want to find under the tree. I decided I'd get him the perfect present. I scraped together $350 and bought him a one-way ticket to Phoenix.

Back then, an airline ticket was a multi-layer, carbonized paper voucher and had to be booked through an agent. Come Christmas Day, that's what my husband found wrapped in a small rectangular box, lovingly topped with a bow. Upon opening it, he looked at me in puzzlement.

"Go see Carol," I (the loving wife) said. "If you want to stay there, stay—but buy your own flight back. Merry Christmas."

He went. It was the best $350 I've ever spent.

The Fifth Principle

We don't always recognize the wrong partner—in relationships or in business. More often than we realize or care to admit, we let the fact that we don't want to "go it alone" colour our decisions. We feel we need something from a partner (usually money or the comforts/security that money buys) beyond the intangibles that are supposed to come with a relationship, such as emotional support, honesty, and integrity. To lock down that security, we shift our thinking and our values, even subconsciously. We let a few uncertainties slide. We settle for less than we truly want—and deserve.

But if we just learn to listen to that uneasy feeling inside, the one that whispers, "Something isn't right," and walk away, if we took a week away to breathe and clear our mind, we might see that doing a one-eighty could save us a lot of tears (and maybe $350).

Forging healthy relationships is the fifth principle of success and it's the one that will likely have the most significant impact on your emotional well-being.

"Marry Well"?

I don't mean marry for money (unless we're talking a lot of money... *Bill Gates money*). I mean really consider the person you choose as a partner. They can make or break your happiness.

Too often, we enter into a relationship—be it business, friendship, or even marriage—because the timing is right. We're looking for money, investors, affirmation, or someone to start a family with, and the person before us seems like The Solution simply because they are the best option at the moment. But are they the best option, *period*? Some of us spend less time auditioning a potential partner than we do looking for a car.

Finding the right partner (in any venture) is one of the most important decisions you'll ever make. Do your due diligence, don't rush your decision, and once you've narrowed the search down to one, go with your gut. If something tells you that you're making the wrong decision, run.

Fast!

But What If I Already Made a Bad Choice?

What if we find ourselves with a complete jerk? What we tend to do (and I am guilty of this as well) is sugar-coat our reality. We look for the good in the other person and we make the relationship "work" (read: continue) because:

- the kids need stability
- we're afraid to be alone
- it's too expensive to leave

- the status quo is convenient
- we're afraid of the future

What that list fails to consider is that we're only given one life to live. Just because we have somehow erred in our choice of partner, just because we have committed to someone whom our saner self would avoid at all costs, it doesn't mean we should try to fix a relationship that is clearly broken or destructive so that "he won't leave." Sure, it can be good for the moment, but in the long run it's a bad choice. We can choose to make a better one.

How We Trick Ourselves: A True Story

Even Before Carol (BC), I suspected my husband was cheating. There were all the clichéd signs. Late nights out. Women's phone numbers on his desk. His repeated declaration of "I never promised to be faithful." He was nothing if not unsubtle.

Given the tenuous fidelity in my marriage, I spent a considerable amount of time pondering my next course of action. So one night, when my wayward husband stumbled home at one o'clock in the morning and greeted me in his usual jovial way, I was prepared—I had flash cards. Ten twelve-by-twelve-inch cards placed neatly, face down, in front of me as I sat cross-legged on our bed.

"Where were you?" read the first.

He looked at me and said (with a smile), "Seriously?"

With no expression (this was in the early nineties—pre-Botox, I might add), I silently held up the next card: "Again, where were you?"

Now he was amused. He decided to play along. "With Brian," he responded.

Next card: "I don't believe you."

His response: "Oh, come on, Ann. Stop it."

You're so predictable, jerk, I thought as I played the next card. "No, I won't stop it."

We went through all ten cards that night, one after the other, each correctly predicting his response. By the end of that unspoken interrogation, he was laughing, I was laughing. I knew him so well and, for all his faults, he got my humour and was ignited by the cleverness. That night, I turned a desperately sad situation into a bearable one, and we were able to find peace in the marital bed. Forget that I was likely seconds. In my mind, I would be the one to win him over (after all, he married me—I got the prize).

Pathetic or familiar?

We were separated within six months. Again peacefully, but without the cue cards. I was suddenly a single mom, with two toddlers and no money.

Cue the next card: "I'm scared."

Sound Familiar?

Maybe you didn't have flash cards. Maybe your relationship ended with more of a bang than a whimper, but the outcome is the same. We try to fix people and we wait too long to leave. We waste time trying to repair doomed relationships when in many cases the writing was on the wall before the ink was dry. But we refuse to see them—until the smoke clears, until the wart is removed, until we are an insecure mess.

Let me say this once (well, I have been married a few times, so maybe twice): You cannot change someone. You cannot control their values. You cannot live someone else's life. You don't exist to cover up or fix someone else's deficiencies, abusive behaviour, or insecurities. What you can do is move on. You will survive—and when you come out on the other side, you won't look back.

Cue the next card: "BYE, FELICIA."

Then exit stage left.

Let's Talk about Divorce

Did you know that Dr. Phil has been married before? Here's a guy who is paid to dole out advice on television, often about relationships. Aren't those types of people supposed to have it all figured out before finding the right partner, to be holding out until they swipe right on their destiny at the age of forty? Does this mean Dr. Phil is not qualified to give marital advice?

I don't know. But he gives sound advice, seems focused on his family, and survived a first marriage. I can't speak to the reason Dr. Phil's marriage dissolved, but as someone who has walked down the aisle a few times, I can sum up the end of a marriage in two words: divorce sucks.

Ending a relationship takes a heavy emotional toll. It forces you to rethink your life, your future, and your past decisions. "Am I good enough?" "How will I survive?" "Why did this happen?"—all the things we really don't have answers for. What I can tell you is that:

1. Yes, it sucks.
2. You will survive.
3. Get your roots done, because life is not over.

The same tenets also apply to ending relationships in business, as well as with friends, acquaintances, and associates.

No Partner Is Better
Than a Bad Partner

After almost every talk or lecture I give, I have a lineup of people (usually young women) who want a few minutes alone to chat. Something I've said makes them want to open up to me. They are excited, they feel their life is ahead of them, but (that big "but!") they have a partner who wants them to go in another direction (e.g., have children, stay at home).

Why?

All of that possibility, all of that desire (or they wouldn't have come to my talk), and they are feeling conflicted about reaching their full potential because their partner has other ideas for them.

Let me be clear: When you have a goal, a passion, or a desire, you are going to have to work to fulfill it. If your partner is not on board, if your partner does not support you (and your goal does not necessarily have to be a "good one"), if your partner chooses to judge you or to guilt you or to offer *anything other than encouragement*, then you have the wrong partner. And you know what else? You are looking to someone else to be your strength, when you should be looking into yourself.

Your partner should support your dreams, encourage you to find your purpose, and give you the freedom to fulfill your potential. A good partner will not diminish your focus with a different agenda or weigh you down with criticism. They will be a positive influence, an encouraging force, a sounding board. If you find yourself gravitating to the wrong types of people, you need to be self-aware enough to seek out support systems (a therapist helps) and surround yourself with people who help you stay on the path of success.

No partner is better than a bad partner.

People Will Get in Your Way

> I remember being fourteen years old and making
> a pact with myself. I would never join into the matrix,
> never join into the status quo, and I would always
> fight. It always felt like I was on an operating
> table and the anesthesia didn't work.
>
> RUPAUL

Romantic partners are just one potential hurdle of the human variety. People, in general, will get in the way of your success— *if you let them.*

Sometimes it's easy to spot the toxic influences in our lives, the people undermining our efforts or even actively working against us. If you're in an abusive relationship or are close to people who bring you down, you already know these individuals are not part of your support system. But not every saboteur in your storyline is a villain. Some of the people poisoning the well of your success may be your beloved friends and family. They may even have the best of intentions, albeit misguided ones.

The Well-Meaning Saboteur

Ironically, the people who most wish for your success are often those most likely to impede it. Friends and family may encourage you in a direction that is "safer" or suggest a path that more closely mirrors the norm (or, more precisely, *their* norm), because they're genuinely concerned about you and have a lower tolerance for risk and/or change.

While well meaning, these people can derail your success by planting seeds of doubt that make you question your choices and ability. To free your mind and unlock your unique personal power, you need to consciously tune out the advice of doubters and remove that obstacle from your path.

The Dream-Killers

An equally detrimental group are the dream-killers. These are the people who tell you, "It can't be done." Or "I just don't see it."

Dream-killers don't show up in dressed in black with wide nets to cast. Quite the opposite: they are almost always someone close to you who feels threatened by what you are trying to accomplish. When someone senses a change in you, when they see you evolving and becoming empowered, they may fear that you'll leave them behind as you move into territory outside their comfort zone. Because they don't think like you, they may not understand your motives or intentions, and they find it easier to try to hold you back than to progress with their own life.

Dream-killers express that insecurity by undermining you in subtle ways. They may encourage conversation for the purpose of debating your choices or move you into a defensive position. They may zero in on your shortcomings, as though it's their job to remind you what you "cannot do." Or they may try to discredit you because:

- they feel you are going to leave them in the dust
- they think it was easy for you
- they think you did something illegal to get where you are
- they believe you slept with someone to get where you are

- they want to be you
- they want to tell you how you can do better (with them in the picture)

Trying to change the mind of someone who feels threatened by you is an exercise in futility. You can be extremely successful in life and entirely self-made, and they'll still sit on their patio on a summer's day telling anyone who will listen, "I said it all along, she slept with Harvey Weinstein—that's how she made her money!" There is nothing you can do with these people but set them down on a bench along your path and wave goodbye to them as you move forward with your life.

Do Not Make Unworthy People a Priority

If you recognize that someone is holding you back and that person is significant in your life, you have two choices: kick them to the curb or manage their influence in your life. In either case, you need to take control of the situation. The only answer that is *not acceptable* is to do nothing.

Start with an audit of your friends, family, romantic partners, business relationships, and even clients. If you feel blessed by the people around you, thinking about their impact and influence on your life will only reinforce your gratitude for them. It'll help crystallize in your mind the positive ways in which they contribute to your well-being. If, on the other hand, you get a sinking feeling whenever you're around someone, if you dread answering their calls, or if you feel bad about yourself after you've spent time with them, it's time to say goodbye. Purge for good.

(It's worth noting here that silence is not sabotage. You may find that the most important people in your life lend an ear but might not comment on your aspirations. That can feel as if they are not helping you make a change, as if you're not being supported, but it's not the same thing as someone getting in your way. Just because someone doesn't support you in the way you want doesn't mean they're a toxic influence.)

Staying on the path to success is difficult enough without people tripping you up. It's up to you to weed out the toxic influences in your life. If your mindset is positive and you are guided by your value system, the right decisions will be clear.

What about Family?

Most people stick with the types of people they knew growing up. These people may be in our lives because they're family (spoiler: we don't all have great families) or because we met them through school, work, or shared interests. We feel that we owe a part of ourselves to these historical ties, even when we no longer share any common interests or values. We say things like, "He's my brother," "He's like a brother," "I need to bail him out, he knows my brother." If we allow ourselves to, we get held back by the people we love. We get stuck in guilt and obligation, which prevents us from growing as individuals, and we remain in a place that ultimately justifies why we never left.

Or, even worse, we grow up in an abusive environment and spend our lives:

- still there
- getting over it/perpetually recovering

- checking in now and then but hating it
- showing up on Christmas Day with a plane to catch at 4 p.m.

If a name popped into your mind as you read that list, then you may be allowing someone to hold you back. But you can choose to move forward. As difficult as it is to have grown up in an abusive home, it's within you to seek the supports you need to work through those complicated emotions and move forward to a more positive, peaceful, and successful future. Save the looking back for bus drivers and accountants. Leave your negative past in the past. Your mom will still be your mom, your brother will still be your brother. *You* can be the change.

Create Room for Success

I look at relationships through a business lens: the best way to end them is logically and practically. If you're in a relationship with someone who you feel is not nurturing you, then get out calmly and pragmatically, just as you would if you were ending a business relationship. You tie up loose ends, you shake hands, pat each other on the back, and say, "It was good while it lasted. Best of luck, let's keep in touch." Oops, also: "If you ever need anything..." Then you move on. You don't have to leave in anger. You just have to leave.

If you're not in a position to push a negative person out of your life entirely, learn to manage that relationship so that it does the least amount of damage to you. Limit the time and energy you devote to them. Refrain from discussing your dreams and aspirations with people who don't have the capacity to support you. Send love and goodwill in their direction, but do it from a safe distance, well out of reach of the ne'er-do-wells trying to suck up your time, bring you down, and/or piggyback on your ambition. Save the negative people you simply cannot get rid of for the commercial breaks; don't give them starring roles in the movie of your life.

There are people out there, amazing people, who will support your dreams. Your next step is to find them. Only positive, supportive people should accompany you on your path.

I know your next question. The answer is: no, people don't change (#pdc).

Find Your People

Everyone needs a support crew to help them along their path, like-minded individuals who aspire to be the best version of themselves and want the same from the people around them. You need to find yours. These people may be family, friends, romantic interests, or business partners. They may have different career goals and aspirations, work in different fields or not at all. They may live in different parts of the world or come from completely different walks of life. The important thing is that they share your desire to pursue a life of success and are a positive influence as you pursue yours.

Your posse may start with just you, right now, or it may be already overflowing with interesting and accomplished people. Ideally, over time, your circle of positive influencers will grow. The better you become at recognizing supportive people, the better you'll be at attracting them into your life; what's more, they'll want to be there. You'll find people you want to draw from, people you trust can get the job done, even if that job is simply advising you on your next step or holding your hand in support.

You want to collect these people and add them to your team. You also want to become enough of an expert to know when you have an original, a rarity, or a fake. I gravitate toward people who are kind, intelligent, happy, and gracious. I thrive on intelligent conversations and can join the best of them in a good laugh or a fun moment. But I also recognize when I have spent time with someone who did not make me feel right. Knowing when to cut ties or, in this case, leave someone "out of your collection" is as important as meeting the right people.

Less is more. But none is too little.

Relationships Are Your Greatest Resource

When I started out in finance, I didn't have the relationships or the resources to support my vision. In many ways, I was completely unprepared and raw. The only helpful things I possessed at the time were a black suit, a white shirt, a cellphone, and a business card that read "Ann Kaplan, Finance." (At least I was official.) What got me through that first year was a numbers game. It was calling, forming relationships, meeting people, and asking for referrals. I started with the phone book, boldly calling up [random industry person] to request a five-minute face-to-face, and ended up in front of the CEO of a bank. There may have been 500 people in between, but I got there.

My goal with every meeting was to a) get enough of an investment that most of my business would be covered for life or b) get a referral to someone who might bring me closer to realizing goal a). Either way, I would not come out empty-handed. What I did not do in those meetings was go off agenda. Whatever I said was the purpose of the meeting was, in fact, the purpose of the meeting. I did not request an informational meeting and then ask for money. I did my research, targeted the accomplished strangers I wanted to have in my fold, and worked to establish relationships with them.

Then I followed up after every meeting with a handwritten thank-you note or a small token to express my appreciation. (I want to be remembered, because I will call again.) I built my network the hard way—one relationship at a time.

The Rules of Engagement

There are opportunities to build your network all around you—at work, at networking dinners, at conferences, at the coffee shop. You just have to be willing to make the effort. Take an interest in the people you meet. Be curious about what they do, how their business works, what's important to them, and take notes. I jot down details on the back of business cards and add short blurbs in the notes of my contact list. I collect people—helpful, smart, interesting people who could potentially be of assistance to me in the future and, if nothing else, are fascinating people to know.

Anyone will hand out their card if they:

a) feel there is a trade
b) find you interesting
c) know you will not stalk them
d) have a "junk mail" filter

The only secret to growing your network is being sincere and engaging. It also helps to remember the following:

1. **Successful people are not stupid.**
The more successful someone becomes, the more others want access to them—for a bit of their fairy dust, for advice, or, God forbid, to take a selfie. Over time, the sheer volume of these demands can make successful people protective about how much of themselves they're willing to share. It also makes them very adept at recognizing people they cannot waste time on. Old friends of the newly successful often fall into this category.

Just because you knew someone in the past doesn't mean you have access to their money/brain/resources. It means you knew them in the past. So if you happen to get your toe in the door playing that card, make sure your pitch is authentic, you have disclosed your agenda in advance, and you are well prepared. Do not assume the recipient is looking to do you any favours or will like your idea because, well, hey, it's you.

If you're smart, you will leave your successful friend to be just that—successful. Cheer them on, don't assume you're entitled to their fairy dust, and stay "old friends."

2. **Successful people are just that—people.**
You need to value them. Think of your relationships as currency: you want to keep them in a safe place until you need them. You also want to be prepared to invest your time, energy, thoughts, and connections into the relationships you desire in your life. Or risk losing them.

3. **Success attracts success.**
Successful people attract each other like magnets. And it's not about money (necessarily); it is about being exceptional

at what you do. You can be a comedian or an actor, in sports or academia, but if you have the drive and focus to be successful "unto yourself," successful people will recognize that quality in you because they recognize it in themselves.

They will also smell a rat—the hovering husband, the insecure wife, the problem brother lurking in the shadows who could make things complicated. You don't have to be rich to be interesting. You do have to be authentically you. (Just don't be authentically you then stalk someone.)

Lessons from My Ex

If going through a divorce taught me anything, it's how to spot a relationship that is destined for failure.

Several years ago, I was invited to attend a meeting with an investment firm. Now, this meeting was of particular importance: It was with the board of directors of a big firm—a game-changing, get-us-on-your-team-and-you-will-never-look-back investment firm. I had been casting for this one in particular for years. They came with experience and credentials and money—lots of it. Together, we'd be a groundbreaking combination.

At the time, I was already established in my field, meaning I'd faced enough rejection to know what *not* to do. I'd also been around long enough to know that when a board invites you to a meeting and says, "Don't bring your CFO, don't bring anyone else, we would like to meet you," they mean business—their minds are made up and that meeting will be the handshake. I didn't just smell victory, I tasted it.

On the appointed day, I arrived a few minutes early. The offices were ostentatious, exuding wealth and success. I wondered

"I GUESS THIS MUST BE PRETTY INTIMIDATING."

if the firm's clients (the ones with the money being reinvested) were as successful as the firm. At the front desk, I was greeted by a polite, if severe-looking, young woman, who escorted me to an empty boardroom large enough to house a small village.

I was advised to take a seat in one of the forty-odd chairs and told that the board would be with me shortly. Ms. Bun-Too-Tight provided a bad cup of coffee to keep me occupied.

I sat there, twiddling my well-manicured thumbs. Five or so minutes later, the board assembled—a line of men seemingly arranged in order of most senior to most junior and, as it so happened, from shortest to tallest—and wove their way around the table toward where I sat. I stood, of course, only to realize how much I towered over the first gentleman, who happened to be the chairman.

With a firm handshake, he looked up at me and said, "I guess this must be intimidating."

Ever the professional, I smiled politely back, peering down on his balding, bespectacled head, and replied, "Sir, I will try not to intimidate you further."

They were not the right fit. I knew better than to try to make that relationship work.

The Bottom Line

The path to success can be lonely. Or, to put it differently, you will be alone on this journey. It is "your path": it's up to you to take ownership of building healthy, supportive relationships in your life; to be accountable for your actions and reactions; and to make positive changes within yourself, not to change others. You are attempting the impossible if you try to change other people. (If you manage to do it, please find my ex-husband and apologize for me—maybe he could have changed!)

Only one person on this planet has the power to create your happiness—*you.*

EXERCISE 8: The Beginner's Guide to the Numbers Game

How to grow your network in six time-tested steps:

1. **Start calling.** Make appointments with people. Ask for five minutes, in person, to pick their brain for advice, and meet at their office. You want to remove all barriers to getting your foot in the door (asking for money or more time or having them come to you are barriers to that "yes").

2. **Be prepared.** You have five minutes. Make the most of them by being prepared. Do your research and write down your questions. Have an agenda for whatever you want to discover or pitch.

3. **Dress the part.** Back in my day, it was the black suit. Today, I believe the lack of a black suit (call it the "anti-suit") is what's in. Apparently, the less you try, the more successful you look.

4. **State your goals.** When you meet, have one goal in mind: you will not walk out of that meeting empty-handed. Ideally, you want to leave with one or all of the following:

   a) a new contact
   b) a referral to someone else who can help you
   c) a follow-up meeting

Make sure the person leaves the meeting knowing you and your goals. 5. Follow up. Send a thank-you note.

6. **Repeat steps 1 through 5 indefinitely.**

Teach a man to fish
and he'll feed his family.
Give him a net
and a canning plant
and he'll feed a village.

(9)

MONEY MATTERS (AND WHY IT'S OKAY TO BE RICH)

Money is only a tool. It will take you wherever you wish, but it will not replace you as the driver.

AYN RAND

WHEN YOU'RE A woman of means, it's commonly assumed that financial success somehow "found" you—that it's something you were born into, married into, or (better still) slept your way into. First, let me say, men are not that stupid (well, most of them), and second, women aren't that pathetic. I'm living proof that it's entirely possible for a single mother with few financial resources to build a billion-dollar business (yes, that's a *b* there) off grit, sweat, and determination. Anyway, I was too homely for anyone to take notice—I had to do it on my own. (*Kidding.*)

The Western world is rife with examples of individuals who have come from nothing and built truly extraordinary businesses and lives—Starbucks founder Howard Schultz, Oracle's Larry Ellison, legendary trader-cum-philanthropist George Soros among them. These individuals own their success... and they can afford to own a lot. It's entirely within the realm of possibility that you can too. I'll even give you the financial blueprint to do it.

The Sixth Principle

Committing to eat, pray, love, and mind our mindfulness is all well and good unto itself, but if we are not considering our financial self, then we aren't looking at the whole picture. Even *Housewives* need to be cognizant of how we support our chosen lifestyle and, what's more, we need to be realistic.

I am not saying money is everything, but that old saying "it sure helps" comes to mind. How nice would it be to not worry about whether you can afford your bills or claw your way out of debt? The answer is, *really* nice. Being financially stable is a fundamental part of living a successful life and it's the sixth principle in this book.

For some reason, though, this is one area that tends to get glossed over when we talk about personal wellness—as if money is evil or unsavoury, or it can only be made by doing something untoward. It's okay to want to be healthy and feed our souls. People pray for food to put on the table and some are even willing to pay for love (or at least the pretence of it). But aspire to be wealthy? Leave that for the rich! In all the emphasis on nurturing our spirit, our health, and our family, we discount the very thing that can make tending to those matters easier for everyone: financial well-being. You can't balance your life if you are overwhelmed by debt, living beyond your means, or oblivious to what it would take to wake up without that added stress.

Dare to Dream

Food on the table, clothes on our back, and a roof over our head—at the bare minimum, financial independence is the ability to meet these basic needs. But it can be so much more than that. With financial success comes the freedom of choice, the ability to make change, and the means to give back. Achieve great financial success and you'll be able to enhance every aspect of your life.

To conceive that opportunity, you need to tap into your creative brain. Real wealth comes from the ability to create: our capacity to take an idea, the starting point of every great achievement, and turn it into something that generates revenue. So, when you ponder what you want in life, why not dream of doing what you love *and* making exorbitant amounts of money doing it? Why put limits on what can be attained? Why not consider all that you could achieve?

The Secret Sauce

Setting out to make money is not the issue; you do that every time you head into work. The issue is wrapping your head around making *a lot* of money—or having a lot of money. It's about understanding that mentality and putting it into action. It's a formula, that secret sauce. With it, you can become wealthy.

If, on the other hand, you want to make the same amount you are currently making, then keep doing the same thing you're doing now and skip to the next chapter. (Kidding, that's a terrible idea.)

Step 1: Think Limitless

When I look back on the lectures I have given about making money, the articles I have written, and those that have been written about me, I can say with certainty that the I advice I gave twenty years ago is the same I'd give today: *think big*. The only limitations to where you can go or how big your business can grow are those you put on yourself.

The biggest mistake I made (let's call it the biggest "learning experience") when I started my business was limiting its possibilities. I dreamed of growing a "million-dollar company." Granted, at the time, I was starting at zero, and a million dollars was a long way off; I just wanted to get off the ground, to have even one customer. I wasn't thinking about expanding into other verticals, investing in real estate, or diversifying outside my core business. Sure, I thought big(ish). But if I had dared to dream even bigger in those early days, if I had thought about how to compound my business as it grew, I could have reached much greater financial heights and sooner. *Hindsight is a bitch.*

Whether you are starting a dog-walking business or climbing the corporate ladder, the most important step in achieving financial success is to remove the barrier of limited thinking. The mindset that sees no limits is open to infinite possibilities. When you start to think bigger (and a little longer-term), you will find yourself working toward goals of scale—asking questions, doing research, and opening up your world to what could be. Don't do the math to figure out how many widgets will make you *x* dollars. Instead, think about how you're going to scale up your business, how to increase the value of your offering, and how to make more money with the assets you already have.

When you begin to dream without limits, your thinking process will change. Your tolerance for risk will grow. You will be focused, energetic, and passionate. Once you adopt a "how can I get there?" mindset, you'll find yourself heading in that direction.

Sounds too simplistic, right? It's not. People strive toward that which they know. A house in the neighbourhood where they grew up. A new SUV. That dream vacation. They'll go into debt or save for years to attain those goals. But if you adjust the picture of "success" in your mind, you'll automatically move the goalpost—and set your expectations accordingly. Start by envisioning what a large amount of money could do for you. Picture yourself in a villa in France, fishing off the Amalfi Coast, or writing a generous cheque for cancer research. Envision yourself in the loftiest of situations, whatever it is that currently seems unattainable, and you'll start to change your habits, your mindset, your spending, and your ambitions to realize them.

Step 2: Focus on Making, Not Spending

Financial peace isn't the acquisition of stuff. It's learning to live on less than you make, so you can give money back and have money to invest. You can't win until you do this.

DAVE RAMSEY

Okay, I just told you to dream of the life you can have with money. In order to get there, though, you have to start living the life you can currently afford. Thinking big does not mean spending big. In fact, in the beginning, do everything you can to avoid investing in that short-term lifestyle (unless it is a means to an end). When you spend, spend with purpose. I'm a tightwad about a lot of things. I make it a habit to always ask for a discount (why pay $10 when you can purchase it for $2?), and I make sure I find value in every dime I spend. For instance, I personally don't feel that wining and dining people is a good use of resources; much can get done in a boardroom, and you don't have to argue over the cheque. Plus, if you ever feel like "that's a lot," then it likely is.

Most people spend their lifetime maintaining a lifestyle, even a less-than-average lifestyle. There is never money put aside for a rainy day (and it *will* rain), and as a consequence there are never enough savings to invest. They live paycheque to paycheque and settle for their lot in life while wishing they had more financial security. Then, when they do make more money, they inevitably spend more, leaving themselves in precisely the same situation but with slightly nicer things. Something's gotta give.

Finding financial peace is as simple as not living beyond your means. It requires being disciplined and committing to either spending less or making more (or both), so you can put money aside. Whether it's cutting up credit cards, not borrowing money, eating in, or doing away with that "little reward" you think you're entitled to after a long week, you need to analyze your budget and architect your spending so that the money coming in exceeds what is going out.

Don't be surprised if you meet resistance to this change in mindset. When we become focused on the cost of everything

"SMART SHOES."

and how we can better monetize our efforts, those who don't think the same way will view us as being "cheap" or "obsessed." Being financially competent and growing wealth is far from both charges—it's being responsible.

Successful people, truly successful people, do not look for other people with money. They surround themselves with intellectuals, politicians, entertainers, and other stimulating people they find interesting. Successful people don't care what's in your wallet or that you can't afford the latest Dior (fictional *Crazy Rich Asians*, aside). They do care if you're posturing as though you can.

Our brains are our greatest accessories, not our shoes.

The Cost of "Free"

The same commitment to responsible spending also applies to business. In any start-up, there is always a period when there is no income—before that first sale, before you have distribution. While you're in that stage, figure out how to cut your personal expenses. Look for ways to keep your costs down. Negotiate everything, and outsource all you can to lower your overhead.

At the same time, remember nothing is free. *Nothing.* Often, we think we're getting a deal or someone is doing us a favour (oldest sales trick in the book), but every interaction, every exchange comes at a price. It's best to cut through the crap and get right to the point of "what will this *actually* cost me?"

Understanding your costs both upfront and in the future will help you make informed decisions. Take a step back from anything that involves cost—whether it's payable in partnerships, money, exchange, or expectations—and think deeply about the offer before you commit. Do not be afraid to ask, "what do you expect in return?" and reiterate how you understand the terms.

Your financial brain must be a creative brain. Your financial brain must accept that you cannot put the cart before the horse—not because it doesn't work, but because you can't actually afford the horse or the cart. Make a plan, look for solutions, and be responsible for every financial decision you make. Keep your head down and your wallet shut.

Step 3: Create Value

. . . .

Money is usually attracted, not pursued.

JIM ROHN

. . . .

Why do some people make more, have more, and even get away with charging more than others? Why does one person keep getting promotions over their co-workers?

The reason, generally, is that *they add more value*. A dependable, skilled employee (or goods and services provider, for that matter) who understands how to increase productivity or sales is worth their weight in gold to a business owner. So, if you really want to make more money, start by demonstrating how you can create more value for your employer or your customers. Show them how you can cut costs, reach more people, increase productivity, or boost sales. Identify problem areas in their business and come up with solutions to improve or fix them. And when you do, discuss how you can increase your compensation as well. Nothing should happen for free.

Step 4: Work Smart

Most people won't make the effort to innovate their workplace. Most people will say, "But I already work long hours" or "I don't want to rock the boat" or "I just need to put food on the table." It's not an either/or situation. You don't have to work longer to make more. You do have to work smarter.

The greatest fortunes are made by individuals who have found a way to scale their ideas and connect with a large audience. We see this in social media influencers, and we see it in the success stories of entrepreneurs such as Bill Gates, Mark Zuckerberg, and Elon Musk. They don't have more hours in the day than you. Larry Ellison and Oprah Winfrey didn't start off with more money or resources than you. They scaled their ideas and their bank accounts by making the most of the time and resources available to them.

So can you. Consider what you know, do what you love, and figure out how you're going to reach the masses. Don't limit yourself to thinking about what you can do within twenty-four hours on any given day (if you don't sleep). You can't create more days or more minutes or eliminate sleep. You *can* create more value. And when you do, more money will follow.

Step 5: Get Financially Literate

Are you financially literate? Most people aren't. But once you're aware of a gap in your understanding, it's up to you to fill it. (FYI, this your cue to start!) When I set out to start a finance company, I knew it was up to me, and me alone, to learn everything possible in order to build a successful business. As the business grew, I realized there were three things that needed most of my focus:

1. Finding solutions
2. Keeping costs down
3. Reaching the masses

By focusing on these three areas, I found new opportunities within my business model. Once I had a solid customer base for my core business, the opportunity to add other products presented itself, which in turn led to still more opportunities to expand. I began to look at each line item on the financial statement as a potential revenue stream:

- Providing insurance = referral revenue opportunity
- Marketing = referral fees
- Providing credit assessment = business spinoff
- Cash flows = potential investment source
- Staff wages = an opportunity to invest in, retain, and encourage great employees (a business's biggest asset!) who can help grow the business further

And I did it. I took cash flows and built a large real estate portfolio based on my ability to service mortgage payments. I created a revenue-generating insurance business based on premiums that were already being purchased by my customers. And I continue to invest in great people (amazing people!)—all the while thinking, *There are no limits.*

Get into the headspace of the financially literate. Ask questions, take courses, ask for five minutes of someone's time. Once you start to understand how the financial world works, you can start making it work for you.

Step 6: Invest, Then Reinvest

The key to making money is figuring out how to scale your business using what you already have, without your direct hands-on involvement. This trick is played in real estate, using portfolios of cash and income as assets to borrow against and reinvest. You don't have to flip your house or sell your business to make more money. Once you have increased its equity, you can borrow against your business (or home) and reinvest in other properties, businesses, and assets to create more wealth. Compounding is a simple formula if you take the time to understand what is required, and it's a proven way to scale your wealth.

The Money Formula

> **It costs less to pursue a life of value than to value a lifestyle you pursue . . .**
>
> ANN KAPLAN

When I first started in business, I was on a spiritual path (which apparently is incompatible with wealth) and trying to put food on the table for my kids. I didn't necessarily think about having money. I did think about the lifestyle money could provide, and while I wasn't sure how I would get there, I knew I didn't want to stay stagnant (and broke). So I widened the path. I focused on my financial health: I made sure I was meeting my obligations to my family, I scrimped and saved and invested in my business, and, when the opportunity arose to diversify, I seized it—as I continue to do every day.

Financial independence, and even great financial wealth, is within the reach of anyone willing to limit their spending and broaden their thinking.

EXERCISE 9: Six Steps to Financial Success

I showed you how I used the six steps to amass wealth. Now, apply them to your own life.

1. **Think limitless.** Start imagining how your dream or idea could grow without any of the barriers currently in your way.

2. **Focus on making, not spending.** What can you do right now to rein in your costs? To make more money? Make a budget and start tracking your spending and planning your savings.

3. **Create value.** Think in solutions. How can you help your employer or customers cut costs, reach more people, increase productivity, or boost sales? What problem areas in their business can you solve or fix? How can you add value?

4. **Work smart.** Working harder doesn't mean working longer. Don't think in terms of the hours you put in but of the value you can add.

5. **Get financially literate.** Do you understand financial statements and investment strategies? Now is the time to brush up on your weak spots. Look for courses online; schedule meetings with financial advisors at your bank. Learn everything you can about finance, so you can make informed decisions.

6. **Invest, then reinvest.** Now execute your strategy. How can you leverage your existing assets to scale your business and your bank account?

NOW GO OUT, kick ass, and get rich!

(III)

SUCCESS
IN ACTION

It's funny...
the harder I work,
the more I achieve,
the more often people tell me
how lucky I am.

(10)

"WORK" IS A FOUR-LETTER WORD, SO IS "CRAP"

Life is too short to fear flying higher.

RICHARD BRANSON

KNOWLEDGE IS POWER—*but only if we put it to use.* Understanding the six principles of success, the potential roadblocks in your way, the importance of believing in your journey, and the necessity of putting negative influences behind you will give you the formula for a successful life. It's up to you to apply it—and yourself—to make success happen.

Once you make that leap and commit, you are on the path and all barriers are behind you. But as the David Bowie song goes, *It ain't easy*. Stepping on the path will put you in the right direction, but it takes work—hard work—and hard work comes with no guarantees (though it certainly improves your chances).

Success is pursued. You have to *learn* what it takes and then *do* what it takes for the pieces to fall into place. The harder you work, the better your chances.

Working It

> ## The reason so few people are successful is that no one has found a way to sit down and slide up hill.
>
> W. CLEMENT STONE

I feel as if I am in an amazing position in my professional life. I choose how I spend my time and don't have worry about putting food on the table. But I work like I am not in this privileged position. I'm still working hard every day to stay on my path. Partly because I enjoy what I do, but also because I worked *really* hard to get where I am and I know that the harder I work, the more I will achieve.

That "really hard" part is what you should pay attention to because it's the stumbling block that trips up most people. You don't have to be the best, the brightest, or the most talented to build a successful business, career, or life. You do need a strong work ethic. Achieving any ambitious goal requires effort—sustained, persistent, dogged effort. You have to work at it, then work at it some more, and, once you achieve some semblance of success, you have to work hard in new and different ways to maintain it.

That doesn't mean you have to work *all the time* or that the work has to be stressful and unpleasant. Working hard and working smart does not necessarily mean working longer hours. If you're in a field you love, work is a pleasure! It can be challenging (in the best way) and, at times, even difficult (in not the best way), yet still be incredibly fulfilling—*if you work at it.*

"Work" Isn't a Curse Word

It is not because things are difficult that we dare not venture. It's because we dare not venture that they are difficult.

SENECA

I consider work a privilege. I feel extraordinarily grateful to work each day with the team of people that I do and for the opportunity to pursue new and interesting projects. But for a lot of people, "work" is a bad word, one with negative connotations. If you find yourself thinking, *It's too much work!* or *Ugh, I have to go to work today,* chances are you're not in your dream job. And you may have a litany of reasons why you think you should stay put:

"That's Just Not for Me."

Many of us focus on what we *don't* have. We see others flourish—get promotions, a new car, renovate their kitchen—and we feel envious but then push away that uncomfortable feeling by convincing ourselves that what we admire and covet is "just not for us anyway." We tell ourselves that we don't need to be rich, we don't need to have a beautiful home, and we don't need to be entertaining or even interesting—that "that kind of lux just ain't for us." Or we rationalize that the sacrifice required to achieve those things isn't worth the effort, saying we won't put in the hours to make more money ("I like my downtime"), won't go on the diet to lose weight ("I like my food"), or won't change our negative tendencies ("Screw it if no one likes me").

We trick ourselves into aspiring for less when what we're really saying is that going after the life we want is "too much effort." There's a word for this feeling: it's complacency and it's a surefire recipe for squelching your dreams. What's great about complacency is that it removes any feelings of guilt. After all, everything is easier when it's *not your fault*. You just couldn't do it. (Because you wouldn't.)

Here's another one for you...

"I'm Content Where I Am."

In theory, contentment is a good thing, right? It's a state of happiness and satisfaction. When you feel content, you have all that you need. There are many areas of your life where contentment is an admirable goal—it's wonderful to be content in the company of your family or your children or your pets. But it's a fallacy to think we're content to accept a lot in life that is less than what we truly desire. That's not contentment. That's giving up.

"I'm Not Lucky."

When someone starts off further ahead in life, with more money and more opportunities, it's easy to attribute their success to the family or the fortunate situation into which they were born. In many cases, that may be a contributing factor, but it alone won't account for their success, and it certainly won't sustain it. Hard work does that. Jan Koum lived on food stamps before he co-founded the mobile messaging app WhatsApp. Italian eyeglasses mogul Leonardo Del Vecchio grew up in an orphanage because his widowed mother couldn't afford to care for him. There are inspiring individuals aplenty who weren't born lucky and yet have realized staggering success.

That's because "luck" and "opportunity" mean nothing if you don't have the ability to deliver—to get the job done, to find the solutions needed, to bring value. *"Luck" is the place where preparedness meets opportunity.*

"I Work for the Weekend."

This last one is perhaps the biggest self-deception of all. The one where we tell ourselves, "Hey, I just do this job so I can book my next trip/golf on the weekend/do the things I actually love." It's a baffling statement. Why in the world would anyone commit to spending forty-odd hours a week doing something they *don't* like so they can afford to devote a few hours at the end of the week to what they do like? If you're going to work, why wouldn't you figure out how to make money doing something that you enjoy? Why wouldn't you want to get paid to pursue your passion?

Sure, you may have transitional jobs in order to work your way to the position you want, but don't let those jobs kill your dream. Those jobs are a means to live your dream. They're not your means, period.

Succeed on Purpose

> **Successful people are not gifted; they just work hard, then succeed on purpose.**
>
> G.K. NIELSON

When you accept that it is *you* who chooses how successful you'll be, when you own that it's your responsibility to figure out what you want and how to get there, you'll open your eyes to the opportunities before you. *Do I need to change my diet to have better skin?* (Is it really that hard?) *Do I need to start working out to feel fitter?* (Okay, that's a half-hour per day.) *Do I need to put in more effort at work?* (If you want a promotion, you do.)

Once you focus on your own life and not on others', once you replace complacency with desire, once you commit to going after what *you* want to achieve, the road map to get there will come into sharp focus. You'll realize it was never the "work" that was the issue. It was the willingness. And what's more, that luck may not find you, but opportunity will. If you're primed to act when your golden chance comes knocking, you can put yourself into a position to be "lucky" too.

Get in the Game

> **I worked half my life to be an overnight success, and still it took me by surprise.**
>
> JESSICA SAVITCH

New England Patriot Tom Brady is widely considered the greatest quarterback of all time. He's one of only two players in history to win five Super Bowls and is a four-time Super Bowl MVP, the most of any player. But Brady wasn't just blessed with incredible passing prowess. In fact, his coach, Bill Belichick, told CNBC's Suzy Welch that Brady "is not a great natural athlete. It is not all about talent; it is about dependability, consistency. If you are coachable and you understand what you need to do, you can improve."

That philosophy is just as relevant in life as it is in football. If you want to achieve the extraordinary—like Brady's incredible 64% pass completion rate—you need to be willing to put in extraordinary effort and not only on occasion. You cannot just do what is expected or meet the minimum requirement—being status quo will not bring you the results you want. You need to take it ten steps further. You need to create the vision, demonstrate the drive, and deliver the results that show others you can not only get the job done but exceed their expectations. The next time opportunity presents itself, you need to be prepared to win.

Persistence Pays

> **I am convinced that about half of what separates the successful entrepreneurs from the non-successful ones is pure perseverance.**
>
> STEVE JOBS

Perseverance is defined by *Oxford English Dictionary* as "persistence in doing something despite difficulty or delay in achieving success." It's a good word to hold in your mind as you work toward your dreams, particularly when you feel yourself start to lose focus.

Impatience is a common obstacle on our path. We don't give success time. We take steps toward the life we want to lead, we earn degrees and certificates, we throw a handful of money at a passion project and say we'll give it "three months, six months... a year," and then we impatiently wait for "success" to appear. We look for signs—that big job, the fancy car, the dream role, the prestigious award—anything that we can hold up as confirmation that we are, in fact, successful. And when those measuring sticks don't appear quickly enough to validate our efforts, we quit. We say, "I tried that and it didn't work," then give up.

Be patient. Give yourself time to make it work. But most importantly, persevere. Stay focused on building what you started and on improving the original design, not on the finish line you haven't yet crossed. Success is not achieved overnight. It's chipped away at daily, one extraordinary effort at a time.

If at First You Don't Succeed

> **Most fears of rejection rest on the desire for approval from other people. Don't base your self-esteem on their opinions.**
>
> HARVEY MACKAY

My son Keaton—likely one of the most grounded, introspective people I know—is an actor. (Brilliant idea, he may just want to be perpetually and justifiably out of work.) I watch him, day in and day out, auditioning for jobs. He regularly books work, but there is a ton of rejection in between. If you think about it, being an actor is the Tinder of occupations—a hundred casting directors will swipe left on your headshot before one takes an interest.

But Keaton never lets that dampen his drive. Every day, he gets up and goes out to be, well, rejected. Every day, he takes another class, he signs up for another improv workshop, he works out and pays attention to his diet; he is constantly honing his craft so he can roll the dice with another audition, knowing that there's a high probability he won't get the part. When I remind him of the commercials and interesting roles he's landed in the past, he inevitably says, "That was yesterday." (He really is his mother's son.) Keaton is always looking to the next project, the next thing he can improve.

And, what's more, he does it with joy.

Keaton faces each day grateful for the opportunity to risk being turned down (yet) again. As his mother, I don't see the rejection he faces, I see the challenge he embraces. Wherever Keaton lands, he will already be successful. He owns his destiny, he works hard toward his goals, and he has no one to credit for his accomplishments but himself. He's either a glutton for punishment or he really does get it.

It's Not Personal

What other people label or try to call failure, I have learned is just God's way of pointing you in the right direction.

OPRAH WINFREY

On the path of success, Keaton is the rule, not the exception. Anyone bold enough to pursue their dreams is going to face resistance along the way. Doors will be shut (even slammed). Unexpected hurdles will pop up (and often at the worst possible moment). Setbacks will occur. The important thing, the way forward, is to turn those stumbling blocks into learning opportunities—opportunities to better ourselves, to polish our pitch, to identify our weaknesses.

To do that, you need to figure out why you were rejected and learn the lesson. At what point did you lose their ear? Was the tone of the meeting wrong? Were the expectations misaligned? Ask what you can do better. And if you get honest feedback, don't lose the lesson to defensiveness. Constructive criticism is a gift rarely bestowed; don't waste it on a bruised ego.

What you should not do is internalize the rejection. If you base your self-worth on the approval of others, you are setting yourself up for a lifetime of disappointment. *Everyone* has an opinion, and sometimes those opinions will not align with yours. So when someone rejects you, particularly if they do it angrily or distastefully, learn from it but remind yourself that this is "their opinion," and if their approach leaves little to be desired, learn from that too. Learning what *not* to do is as important as learning what to improve on.

When you are sure of who you are and live by your values, you won't take rejection personally or let it define you. Sure, occasionally something someone says may get under your skin, but it'll be a minor blight in your day, a necessary evil in pursuing your dreams—not a crushing defeat.

There Is No Substitute for Hard Work

If there was an easy way to achieve success, some clever individual would have found a way to package it up and market it to the masses already—just imagine how much money you could make off a get-rich-quick scheme that actually worked! *But there's not.* And anyone who suggests otherwise is probably trying to sell you something (like a get-rich-quick scheme).

But you *can* get rich. In rare cases, it may even happen rather quickly. But it will not happen without effort. Living a life of success takes time and a tremendous amount of hard work. *It ain't easy.* But it's entirely worth it.

EXERCISE 10: Eight Tips to Work Smarter

You know how to work longer; let's try learning to work smarter.

1. **Believe.** Understand that *you* are the one who can make change.

2. **Be accountable.** You must have a desire to succeed and to succeed by your own hand. No one can do the work for you.

3. **Get inspired.** Money and promotions will not inspire you to work harder, at least not in the long term. You need to find a way to personalize your efforts, to create a sense of purpose to

your goals—such as a better quality of life for you and your family, or the chance to make a real difference in your community or field of service.

4. **Don't waste an opportunity.** Make every action count, and do not pass up an opportunity to contribute.

5. **Practice punctuality.** Be on time (or early). Being punctual is about being present. It tells others you are worthy of their time and they are worthy of yours.

6. **Be professional.** Dress the part but also act it. Be respectful and stay focused on the task at hand and the value you add. Don't ad lib or self-promote.

7. **Organize your time.** Schedule when you will work, when you will leave work, and when you will do all the other tasks you need to accomplish in a day. An organized life is a lot easier to manage and removes from the equation the counterproductive "Where are my keys?" crises and scattered "Where was I?" thoughts. Use your digital calendar to log all your notes, appointments, and deadlines in one location—and one location only.

8. **Work smarter.** Get out of the mindset of clock-watching. Wherever you are working, be and do the best you can—or find another job.

If Google says it's great,
it must be great.
So I created a web page
that says I'm "great."
Now it's official.

(11)

I AM WHAT I AM, I IS WHAT I IS

Life isn't about finding yourself.
Life is about creating yourself.

GEORGE BERNARD SHAW

FOR THE BETTER part of my grade school years, I was the only Asian kid in an overwhelmingly white school in Victoria, British Columbia. I stood out, a visible minority in a sea of Caucasians, and my classmates made sure to point it out on regular occasion. I would arrive to class confronted by "NO-NOSE" and "RICEBAGS" scrawled in chalk on the blackboard. On the playground, kids would hold me down so they could demonstrate just how flat my nose could go, pushing it down while I lay prostrate on the ground. An alternative to marbles and skipping rope, I was a recess recreation and not because of my lively personality.

The parents were little better. Most couldn't understand where this Asian child had come from (both my parents were white) and assumed, almost comically, that I would be challenged by the English language, only ate with chopsticks, or was destined to clean their homes. They weren't sure what to make of me and, in hushed whispers, cautioned their children (my friends) against associating with me. It probably didn't help that I dressed like an extra from *Little House on the Prairie*. If the "pug nose" didn't confirm that I was different, my penchant for large bows, big white collars, and knee-length, plaid dresses did.

"What is she anyway?"

"*Careful.*"

The funny thing was I didn't even know I wasn't white, or that I dressed like a dork. (I liked the bows!) I grew up sitting across the table from my white sisters and parents; I had always assumed that I was one of them. Looking back, the cruel and discriminatory references to my features and skin colour confused me as a child, to say the least, and, sadly, did not stop on the playground. The schoolyard was my first experience with discrimination and I didn't even know I was the target.

The Inescapable Past

When you're a social outcast, it's easy to internalize the hurtful words and negative stereotypes hurled at you. We're told (in words and through actions) that we are of lesser status and we begin to accept it as Truth. We let the labels people put on us mould our view of ourselves. *They say I am, therefore I must be.* The double-edged sword of public opinion slices the other way too. The more positive feedback someone gets, the more they seek validation of their worth in the opinions of others and then bend to meet those expectations. *They say I am, therefore I must be.*

Our pasts shape who we are as adults, and the rare few who manage to rise above the circumstances of their birth are deemed an anomaly—given the odds, they likely are. But we don't have to be who society tells us we are. We can choose how we respond. We can:

- try to ignore what people say
- try to change their minds
- rally against preconceived ideas of who we are

Or we can embrace our personal power and be precisely the person we choose to be. We can recast our role, reject the labels given to us, defy expectations, and create a new blueprint of who we aspire to be and the values we hold dearest.

How? We're going to talk about that in detail, but first let's take a quick trip down the grocery aisle...

Be the Mushroom

Imagine you are pushing your cart down an aisle in Costco and a nice saleswoman summons you over to her sample table to try a tiny enokitake pancake she's just whipped up. A flat blini-sized morsel sizzling at the end of a tiny plastic fork, crispy golden brown strings of mushroom delicately poking through the sides. It looks tempting! You try it. It's warm, palatable. The kindly store-floor chef shows you the box of pancake mix and hands you a package of fresh mushrooms. Why not? You take both.

Something you would never have considered making, let alone buying, on your bulk shopping trip is now in your cart. Those skinny little mushrooms find their way into your home—a (seeming) lifetime supply of fungi looming large on your refrigerator shelf, its expiration date quickly approaching.

That purchase did a little more for you than take up real estate in your fridge. Seeing those exotic mushrooms staged as an appealing finger food changed your perception of what *you* could do. The simplicity of the mix allowed you to imagine a new dish you could add to your cooking repertoire, something you could serve to hungry guests. And it made you feel good. For a few moments, you exchanged pleasantries, broke up the monotony of your shopping trip, and made the saleswoman smile.

Your purchase also satisfied the anticipated response that the Mushroom Pancake Co. had when you passed within three feet of their sample table. Five minutes prior, you wouldn't have considered purchasing those odd-looking mushrooms. In fact, you couldn't even identify them without Google. But you did buy them, and willingly.

Is that all you have to do? Is it that easy to attract people, to influence the way they think about something—by simply changing its packaging?

Celebrities and public figures do this all the time, not with food (Martha Stewart aside) but with the personas they strategically create for themselves. The "package" they present themselves in. We see it in Katy Perry's confection-coloured dresses and in Hillary Clinton's omnipresent pantsuit and wry smirk. They develop an image, dress the part, and then play the role they want the world to associate with them. And we buy into it.

These individuals didn't start off successful and then create their brand. They crafted the image they wanted to project and used it to elevate their platform and, ultimately, to get into your head, heart, and homes—just like those little mushrooms.

But I'm Not a Celebrity

Now you may be thinking, *What does this have to do with me? I'm not famous.*

The truth is, you already have a personal brand. We are creating one every time we post, share, or tweet on social media. It's in your Instagram bio and Twitter handle, defined in 150 characters or fewer. It's in the content of your Facebook feed and the hashtags on your posts. We tell the world who we are with every digital footprint we make.

We do it in the real world too. Your personal brand is reflected in the clothes you wear, the way you present yourself to others, the car you drive, the causes you support.

The question to ask yourself is: What message is your brand sending? Is the picture of your best self consistent with the one you put on Facebook? Is it in line with the goals you want to achieve? By default, we will be ourselves, of course. But take a step back and consider if the public face of "you" is on brand with the values you represent.

When you consciously decide what kind of person you want to be and start taking deliberate steps toward becoming that person, you will be more aware of your words, your appearance, your actions, and the messages they send. Lady Gaga is the poster girl for individuality in all her "born this way" Kermit-the-Frog-dress glory. Oprah Winfrey is the embodiment of self-empowerment and living authentically. Think: what does your personal brand (that you didn't know you had) say about you?

But I Like Me the Way I Am

You might not like the idea of having a personal brand or of thinking of yourself as a brand. But set those misgivings aside for a moment. You don't have to dramatically change who you are (except maybe you do) or adopt a new way of life (unless, of course, you should): a personal brand is really about being aware of how you present yourself to the world.

More often than not, we create a personal brand (without realizing it) and then become stubbornly resistant to changing it (also without realizing it). How many times have you walked into a clothing store only to gravitate toward things you already have in your closet? A little black dress in the same style. The T-shirts, suits, and shoes that are only slightly different from something we've purchased before.

With age, our commitment to "the way things were" only deepens—we get more firmly entrenched in the version of "me" we hold in our heads. Part of it is a rite of passage; we're apt to care a little less about what people think as we get older. But we are also less open to the idea of change. Or to think we need to change in the first place. *I like me the way I am and I'm not changing now, thank you very much.*

In principle, that's great!

Only it may not be *entirely* true. There are two scenarios in life that show us we not only have it in us to change but also have a desire to change: trips to Vegas and visions of retirement.

People of all walks of life step off a plane in Las Vegas and become a more outgoing version of themselves. Somehow the clothing is a little tighter, the mood is a little more jovial, and the wallets are a little looser. People don't go to Vegas to continue doing what they do at home, to continuing being "as they are." They go to Vegas to let loose, to get in touch with another side of themselves, to temporarily change.

Retirement is another time when we embrace change, at least theoretically. We envision ourselves spending more time at the cottage, travelling the world, or playing with our grandchildren. We dream of a life, whether or not we strive to achieve it, where we can relax and enjoy each day without the pressures of work and deadlines and looming bills. We imagine ideal scenarios to be realized at a later date.

Retirement and Vegas tell us that, at least subconsciously, there is another life we want to live. The question is: why are we waiting to embrace that version of ourselves, to rebrand, as it were?

Giving Birth to a Brand

Your brand is what people say about you when you're not in the room.

JEFF BEZOS

When I set out to create my personal brand, I sat down with my PR team and my publicist. Four people in the room. Four different ways of thinking—and me, silently listening to the clock ticking down dollars. (Okay, some aspects of my life are not *entirely* relatable, just bear with me here.) It's an exercise that I feel I already know how to do, that I have learned over a lifetime. (Who knows *me* better than I do?!) But I'm willing to pay for their input because my brand needs to be defined in succinct terms; it was time to decide what I want to be known for—the conception stage of creating a brand.

Over the next few hours, we looked at my history and my experiences. They listened as I talked about what is important to me.

"Business . . . and I am smart," I told them. "I am in finance, I have many degrees in finance, I lecture about finance—I live, eat, breathe finance." It is important to me that I don't lose sight of my business side.

The other side, they piped in, is how I present myself.

"Luxury. You are not Winners."

(I argued, as I do shop there.)

I added one last thing: "Funny."

They looked at me. "Well, kind of funny."

I walked into that meeting a mother, a half-white/half-Asian entrepreneur, a friend, a cook, a wife, and a myriad of other identities I label myself with (correctly or not). I walked out "a luxurious, kind-of-funny businesswoman."

There, that day, a brand was born. It didn't mean that all my other defining roles became null and void. It meant that under the glare of the public spotlight, and in the glow of social media, those three features were the ones I'd let shine. My mission from that day forward was to embody and defend my personal brand.

InstaYou

> Today you are YOU, that is truer than true.
> There is no one alive, that is YOUER than you.
>
> DR. SEUSS

Turns out that coming up with my brand was the easy part; putting it into practice proved more challenging. Take my Instagram page. I struggled to come up with a bio that summed up "me" in 150 characters. I wanted to write "Mother of eight" and "Author" and "Television personality" and "Public speaker" and "Wannabe sculptor" and "Spiritual advisor"— there were so many things that I wanted to include! On the flip side, a part of me thought, *Ha! If I did put these things, people are going to laugh at me. Do I have the right to call myself a "Television personality"? I am not on the A-list. I am going to be trolled by haters!*

I did not like it, Sam-I-Am.

After much deliberation, I ended up with a statement that I believed in: "Whatever you do, whoever you are, own it." It's meant to be an expression about being accountable and self-empowered. I didn't work "luxury" or "business" buzzwords into my bio because I felt those are more about image than me as an individual. But I did add a reference to my job (CEO) and a link to my company's Instagram page. I chose to use words that I could stand by, even if they didn't encompass a global view of my life.

Maybe tomorrow I'll change it to something else.

Build Your Brand

> **We cannot and must not get rid of nor deny our characteristics. But we can give them shape and direction.**
>
> JOHANN WOLFGANG VON GOETHE

You don't have to hire a PR team or a publicist to come up with your personal brand. You do need to spend some time thinking about who you are, about the 150 characters you want to be defined by.

Are you funny (or kind of funny)? Are you an academic? Are you a free spirit? An activist? Are you a homemaker? (Careful not to use the word "housewife" here.) What does successful-you look like? Maybe you can't picture what you'd look like physically, but you can probably envision how you think success will *feel*—is it satisfaction, is it pride, is it fearlessness?

Now, take a step back and ask yourself, "What do I want to be known for? How would successful-me be?" Can you picture that individual without weighing them down with the baggage of your past? This is where we limit ourselves. We fall into the trap of letting the negative events of our past colour the visions we have of our future. Can you break free of the labels others have given you and become a better, bigger version of yourself?

Defining your brand is not about changing anything about yourself, per se. It's about getting a clear picture of the characteristics you want to embody and then tailoring your public image, posts, and person to reflect them. It's also about shedding any unflattering, or even negative, images you may have of yourself and replacing them with an empowering alter ego, one who will help you be the very best you. (Beyoncé named her alter ego Sasha Fierce. Just FYI.)

Now Live It!

> ### The difference between who you are and who you want to be is what you do.
>
> UNKNOWN

Knowing what you want your personal brand to be is half the battle. Figuring out how to embody that brand—to be that person—is what will win the war. Your brand is expressed in how you act, how you dress, what you post on social media, and the way you engage with people. It's in the confidence you project and the honesty with which you live your truth.

By thinking about your brand, you can breathe life into the idea. By describing it, you can decide exactly what it looks like. And by living it, you can become it.

That's not to say it'll happen overnight. If you want to be a savvy and self-confident business person and you currently struggle with anxiety, it's going to take time and effort to build yourself up. If you want to be fit and full of energy and are living a sedentary lifestyle, you are going to have to add more movement into your day.

And that's half the fun. When you take conscious and intentional steps toward being the person you choose to be, you move further along the path to success and closer to the best version of yourself with every stride.

Don't Let Anyone Tell You Who You Are

I grew up ignoring racial prejudices and have moved through life pushing for successes (as I measure them)—writing books, lecturing, earning degrees, and building flourishing businesses. I have accomplished these things not because I am "Asian," not because I am a "woman," and not because of "*him.*" I have achieved them because I am a focused, hard-working, intelligent person who seized the reins and took control of her life. (Also, I have great teams in place.)

Building your brand is more than a personal marketing exercise. It's about taking ownership of your self-image. If you grew up in a repressive environment, one where knowledge or creativity or self-expression were not given an opportunity to develop, or where you were considered "different" and therefore "inferior," or were told "you can't do that" or "you're not good enough," you probably have a limited view of yourself as an adult. Hear something long enough and you're bound to believe it. *They say I am, therefore I must be.*

We build our lives on top of the foundation of those faulty beliefs. We look for jobs within our "limited" capacity. We accept that we should live in a certain area or dress a certain way because that is where we started or what people expect of us. We let society tell us who we are.

But we don't have to listen! It's in our power to reject the labels other people put on us. Building your brand is a tool to take control of that narrative and flip the script, to tell the world who we are, not vice versa—and it's incredibly empowering! If I went by what other people thought I should be, I'd be giving you advice on the best way to get stains out of your carpet right now, not on how to live a life of success. (The answer is Oxi-Clean, by the way. That stuff is magic.)

Change how you think and you will change your world. Why not start now?

EXERCISE 11: Find Your Insta Inspo

In this exercise, you will break down the characteristics of people you admire, dissect what most appeals to you about them, and use it to create your own personal brand superhero—or monster. (*It's alive!*)

A good way to envision the type of person you want to be is to look for role models who already embody those qualities. Who do you admire? And, more importantly, why? What is it about them that appeals to you? This is not an exercise you will share or be graded on, so don't think about how others will judge your list. *It's your list.* It doesn't matter if Britney Spears is your queen or Gloria Steinem is your gold standard: the important thing is that you identify the characteristics that those individuals represent for you.

I, personally, take inspiration from Lady Gaga, Katy Perry, and Hillary Clinton. There are many people who inspire me but, in particular, those three women do. Each one has consciously and strategically created a persona that accurately reflects her beliefs, is instantly identifiable, and is unapologetically herself. You might not like their personas but there's no denying that they exist.

So, who do you want to be like?

Franklin D. Roosevelt said,
"The only thing to fear
is fear itself."
Clearly, he never met
my mother-in-law.

(12)

THE ONLY THING
TO FEAR IS GIVING UP

**Fear defeats more people than
any one other thing in the world.**

RALPH WALDO EMERSON

MOST PEOPLE KNOW me best from my role on *The Real
Housewives of Toronto*. But that wasn't my first time
working in television: I hosted three shows prior. The
Housewives was my first foray into reality TV and, as some-
one who makes a living in finance, it certainly wasn't a call
I was expecting.

Or one that I could have prepared for.

A reality show assessment is a two-part exam designed to
determine if you are the right fit without giving you any idea of
what the "right fit" might be. (Is there a pass or fail grade?) It
starts with a rapid-fire Q&A on camera (the oral exam). From
there, you're sent for a battery of EQ and IQ tests to evaluate

your sanity, smarts, and character—or lack thereof. (If you tease the assessor, will it impact your grade?) I'm not sure how I did on the tests, but they asked me to be on the show. (Did I get it because I passed or because I failed?)

When reality TV came knocking, I swung the door wide open.

Reality Check

Before the *Housewives*, I lived a private life: I never sought the spotlight, never tried to get invited to the "it" party. I really didn't give a hoot about what others thought and was happy living in my own reality.

Those casting tests forced me to take a closer look at my life. All of a sudden, what I had never considered to be measurements of success was pulled out, weighed, and examined under the microscope of reality TV. I felt very exposed during that process, and once the testing wrapped, the inevitable moments of self-doubt followed. *What if everyone hates me? What if they call me ugly? If I get the part, is that even a good thing?* I began to question who I was.

Do I want to do this??

I was keenly aware that if I did the show, my actions would be seen and scrutinized by many—that I was opening myself up to criticism on social media. My children asked me why I would put myself in that position. My friends thought it was hysterical, and the finance world I worked in braced for the impact. But the most important person (I felt) to decide if I should do it was *me*. Aside from wanting to try something new, wanting the adventure, the one factor that made me say, "Yes," was that I was comfortable with who I was. If I was going to play me, I would be me.

The Fear (of Failure) Is Real

> **Courage is rightly esteemed the first of human qualities ... because it is the quality which guarantees all others.**
>
> WINSTON CHURCHILL

A whole host of fears ran through my mind before I signed on for the *Real Housewives*. But that fear was a familiar script—it's a part of life. We live in fear, the vast majority of us. We're afraid of aging, of being alone, of being in debt, and of making the wrong choices. Fear compels us to stick to the status quo (what we know), while in the meantime we go into debt, end up alone, and become all of the things we were afraid we would—*and* we got older in the process.

But perhaps the biggest fear of all is that of judgment. We let our ego get in the way of our success because we're afraid to fail or, more specifically, we're afraid that others will *see* us fail. It's the little voice that whispers, "Don't put your hand up" in class, that stops us from speaking up at the boardroom table. The one that sneers, "They'll laugh at you," or "You don't want to look stupid, do you?" Fear is powerful and, when left unchecked, it can block your path to success.

The truly tragic part is that we let it. We stop investing in ourselves. But with knowledge comes the uncomfortable truth that:

a) we live the life we choose, and/or

b) someone's disapproval may confirm something about us we believe to be true

But, if we choose to set fear aside, we can just as easily clear the path. If you can learn to silence that negative voice in your head, anything and everything you've ever wanted to do will be on the table. When you remove the fear barrier, you open yourself up to raising your hand, to living in the moment, to letting go of the past, to liking yourself for who you are, to love. You seize one moment and then another, pushing fear aside each time, until your life is made up of thousands of moments when you chose opportunity over apprehension. And if some don't work out the way you planned or hoped, you take comfort in the fact that you tried, knowing that more (and bigger) opportunities await you around the corner.

Oh, if only it was that easy.

It is.

Free to Fail

Growing up, I was never a beauty, never the one singled out in high school yearbooks as a "future star," and I certainly didn't come first in anything (except for math, but that just confirmed I was a dork). In all truthfulness, I was so under the radar that any effort I made toward anything would go *unnoticed*. I could fail and no one would even know I was in the race. That freedom to fail made me willing to try anything. It made me unstoppable.

Even now, there's nothing that I wouldn't try. Just the idea of something new and interesting excites me. In fact, it's what drives me. I am not afraid of failing, I am afraid of not trying. Shirley MacLaine aside, we have one—and only one—life to live. I'm determined to live this one to the fullest and make every minute count. That means moving forward all the time, failure be damned.

Failure Is the Mother of Success

Everything is hard before it's easy.

JOHANN WOLFGANG VON GOETHE

Success is not the absence of failure: it's the ability to learn from failure. I wouldn't have been married a few times if I hadn't messed up, somewhere. I wouldn't have learned the power of hard work if I hadn't struggled to build my business. And I wouldn't be telling the truth if I said I'd never done anything petty (like have my husband's ugly plaid shirts taken in so they wouldn't fit him). In order to find success, I had to hit walls, learn not to put all my eggs in one basket, and grudgingly accept lumberjack plaid. (Just kidding. I'm still not a fan.) I had to make mistakes and learn from them—and then I had to mess up in new and different ways to learn more lessons still. And I continue to do so.

You don't have to win to be on the path of success—just putting yourself out there is a step in the right direction. Great artists and athletes are not measured by their first attempts. We don't count how many times young Wayne Gretzky missed the net or how many times Michelangelo's early sketches were critiqued. We marvel at the wondrous things they accomplished because of their relentless commitment to trying, to honing their skills, to taking risks, to pushing past their fears.

The good news is you already have the tools at your disposal to clear a mess off your path and keep moving forward. You'll never know if your next attempt will be the one that puts you on top until you try.

Mistakes Will Be Made

It may have taken a reality show assessment for me to realize I'm comfortable in my own skin, but it was the process of filming that taught me how important it is to live in the moment.

There are no take-backs on reality TV. If you want to be perceived as successful, kind, and thoughtful, then you better act like a successful, kind, and thoughtful person. Wanting to be one way while acting another is not a version of reality you're going to enjoy watching on the small screen. (Any of the *Housewives* can attest to that.)

There were a few moments on the show when I felt I fell short. There's a scene at a restaurant when Kara Alloway and Joan Kelley Walker are having words outside and I suggest that the rest of us take bets on who will win the fight. It was meant to be a joke but, watching that scene on the show, it hurt their feelings. I don't like the way I behaved in that moment, but I have to own it and (hope!) I've learned from it.

What Do You Have to Lose?

The next time you consider taking a risk, ask yourself, *What do I have to lose?*

The trouble with risk and failure is that we tend to think of them in extremes—hanging by a thread from a balcony, jumping from an airborne plane, losing our life savings in penny stocks. But we rarely give that much thought to the consequences of *not* taking a risk.

What about the risk of staying stagnant? Why aren't we afraid of letting success pass us by? Of letting someone kill our dreams? Of winding up twenty years from now thinking *coulda, woulda, shoulda*? Every time you decide to stay in a dead-end job, every time you put your dreams on hold for "just another year," every day you stay in a toxic relationship, you are putting your dream life in jeopardy. Is *that* a risk you're willing to take?

The thing we stand to lose when we roll the dice on ourselves is the very thing we stand to gain. If we do not invest in our idea, we'll never build a successful business. If we do not open our hearts to love, we'll never find our match. If we never step outside our comfort zone, we'll never get on the path of success. The next time you feel tempted to accept the status quo as the *safe* option, consider the cost to your dreams. How much does someone have to pay you to give up on yourself? Is it a raise? A car? A new house? The illusion of security? Is *that* risk worth the reward?

Risk isn't like dangling above shark-infested waters, it's not about "winner takes all" or "life and death." Risk is simply investing in unfamiliar territory. And you've already done it a hundred times before. If you've ever moved out, started a new job, changed careers, gotten married, or had children, you've made a leap of faith that requires embracing the risk of failure. Your desire outweighed your fear of the unknown. The risk justified the reward.

There Is No Road Map

There are no guarantees in life and that uncertainty creates fear. I see it in my own children. They dream of success in their respective pursuits, but they're not sure how to get there and hope that someone will hand them a map of the precise path they need to follow. What they don't yet realize is that they are the ones who create that map; they're in charge of their journey—with all of its risks and rewards.

It's up to each of us to step out of our comfort zone, to arm ourselves with knowledge, experiences, and expertise, and to take a risk on the life we want to live. Most people won't go after their dreams. Most will stick with the status quo. That alone tells us that the *real* risk isn't trying something new. It's giving up before you start.

EXERCISE 12: Five Simple Steps to Overcoming Fear

1. Want something more than you are afraid of it.

2. Thinking will not overcome fear, actions will. Take action.

3. If you fail, that means you tried and hopefully you learn something. Be more afraid to say you didn't try than to say you failed.

4. Trying takes courage. Courage is not the absence of fear but the triumph over it.

5. If you can't beat fear, then do it scared.

Today is your day, the day you
will make the difference.
Today is the day you start
to focus on a new you,
when you realize that your efforts
will not just encourage change,
they will be the change.
Today is the day you throw out
excuses and disbelief,
when you stop looking behind
and start looking ahead.
Today is the day you turn away
from that which holds you back,
when you shut the door to negativity
and open a window to opportunity.
Today is the day you say, "I can!"

(13)

SUCCESS STARTS NOW (WHAT ARE YOU WAITING FOR?!)

Though no one can go back and make a brand new start, anyone can start from now and make a brand new ending.

CARL BARD

W HEN I WAS young, I used to think I was already formed: Who I am is who I will always be. I believed my personality, like Freud theorized, had developed by the age of five and, in the absence of some extraordinary or catastrophic event, I would not change. There—done—I was set.

In my mind, that meant my life was predetermined and, if I pleased my parents, I would marry a doctor (like my father was), have many babies (like my mother did), and buy a house (as my parents had). Accomplish a, b, and c, and I would be deemed "successful."

At just five, my destiny was decided.

And in many ways, it was. The fact is many of us grow up only to recreate some version of the life—happy and loving or not—that we knew as children. We tend to walk in our parents' shoes, carry on their traditions and values, and maybe even follow similar career paths. We set goals: marriage, kids, house (full stop). We strive to reach that predetermined bar. Then when life gets in the way, we feel like we failed. Or worse yet, we allow that failure to be a catastrophic event that defines our self-perception.

Even when we meet "the bar," we sell ourselves short. We spend too much too soon. We chase after things that give us short-term gains, without considering the long-term implications. We take promotions in jobs we don't love and sign contracts that tie us down for years (*I'll start that business later*). Why? Because we want money for something now. Because we want security... now. We settle for mediocrity because the future is uncertain and life is not fair and the alternative— stepping away from the comfort of the *now* to open our lives to the potential of *tomorrow*—seems frightening.

The effect is that we busy ourselves striving for the things we think we *should* be and, in the process, we greatly limit ourselves from all that we *could* be. We try to get on someone else's path, instead of finding our own, and then we're:

a) surprised when it never really leads us to the happiness we desire, and

b) oblivious to the other world out there, the one free of the limitations we set for ourselves.

Only we don't have to be.

Remember, you create your reality... the world isn't what others tell us it is.

Everything around you—what you are wearing, the furniture you own, the smartphone you carry, the coffee shop you frequent—all that we see was created by someone just like you. With dreams like you. With challenges like you. The difference between "the successful" and everyone else is that they stuck to their own path and, entirely unsurprisingly, it took them where they dreamed of going.

Don't waste your life living someone else's. *Not even Freud's.*

Success Is within You

> **The only person who can stop you from your destiny is you.**
>
> ANN KAPLAN

Successful people are deemed a rarity. They're achievers who know "the formula" and, regardless of the task, are looked upon to deliver, to just *get it done*. But true success stories are not measured by singular achievements; we are not defined by a great moment or two. True success is a way of being and it is within each of us, no matter where we start or what our goal—*if* we reach for it.

When you realize that you are the maker of your own destiny—that you have the tools and the mindset to achieve your goals, and that with focus and hard work, everything is within reach—you will not just have hope, you will get excited about the possibilities your life has to offer!

Five Things Success Is Not

> **The moment you take responsibility for everything in your life is the moment you can change anything in your life.**
>
> HAL ELROD

I've taught countless lectures, workshops, and courses on how to be successful. Each time I prep for a talk, I consider the audience and their immediate challenges and long-term goals. What could I tell a group of (already successful) female surgeons that they don't already know? What advice could I give 500 teenagers who have struggled to overcome abuse, abandonment, or addiction? We're all looking for "the answer," we all want hope, and we all want the recipe to realize our dreams. And so the message, no matter the audience, is ultimately the same: being successful is a way of life ... it is not about money, it's a mindset.

Which means ...

1. There Is No White Knight

Success is available to anyone with the desire and drive to create it, but no one can make it happen for you.

We cannot look to other people to create our happiness or fix our problems. There is no white knight waiting in the wings to swoop into your life and fill it with joy, no fairy godmother who will magic your problems away, no financial guru who can make your business into an overnight success. There is only one person responsible for your success—*you*.

That doesn't mean we should be impervious to what makes us *unhappy*. It means taking responsibility for our actions and our reactions, being cognizant of the influences we let into our lives, and being accountable to ourselves.

And once you do, it's incredibly empowering.

2. Your Past Doesn't Determine Your Future

Imagine for a moment that you are a parent and your child is leaving home. You stand at the door as he says his goodbye and steps out into the world. Everything you have done for him up until that moment is behind him. You watch as your child walks off toward the horizon, his sights set on all that lies ahead. That child can go in any direction, but he cannot change where he came from.

The same is true in your life. We cannot change what happened twenty years or one minute ago. Or that we walked down the aisle with the wrong person or that someone jilted us. We cannot take back words or change history, nor do we need to look back or apologize for what we were or where we came from. What we *can* do is choose how we will live tomorrow. Staying focused on our future doesn't mean we don't respect our past or our roots, it means we learn from it. Staying focused is about forging our own way, finding the path that leads to *our* success and staying on it.

3. Success Isn't Stagnant

In the last years of her life, my mother lived in our home. By that time, she was an invalid, unable to walk, and in the late stages of dementia. She had little memory but always retained her strong insight and wisdom. I didn't seek her advice very often: I knew what she would approve of and, if there was ever any doubt, her bedroom was off the main kitchen in our house so she could hear everything and didn't think twice about sharing her opinion—typically with an incredulous "ha!" from behind her bedroom door. (There was no escaping her!)

I lost someone very close to me while my mother was with us, and I was struggling to come to terms with the loss. I had trouble motivating myself and I felt guilty about enjoying life. Tearfully, I sought my mother's advice. Her response has helped me with every loss I have experienced since, and I repeated her words to me in my dedication to her years later when she passed.

"Mom, a friend of mine has died ... I do not know how to handle her loss."

"What would she have wanted you to do?" Mom asked.

"She would have wanted me to be happy." I struggled. "She would have wanted me to carry on with the work she was doing and to look after the people she cared about."

"Then," said my mom, "carry on her good work. Try not to mourn her death but to honour her life."

That advice gave me a tremendous sense of purpose and immense appreciation for the goodness in my mother and my late friend. Sometimes you have to tear a page from the books of those who came before you in order to get back on your path.

4. Success Is Not Material Things

All the money in the world cannot buy you a personality and it certainly will not bring you happiness. Measuring your success by material possessions puts you on the never-ending treadmill of consumption; you have to constantly spend to keep up and will never reach the finish line. When you attach your self-worth to the things that you own, the job that you have, or the house you live in; when you entrust your happiness to superficial objects and meaningless titles, you allow others—or, more precisely, what you believe others to think—to determine your value.

Success is defined by the life you live, not by the material things in it. Happiness is measured by how closely you live your values, not by how much others value you. When you take control of both, you empower your best self.

5. No One Writes the Rules for You

I do not live for my husband; at times I don't even like him. He does not tell me what to do and I don't exist to live up to his or my children's expectations. I try to be a good wife, to be a good mother, and to lead by example. But I live my life by my rules and I hope that my values are such that I am not doing my family a disservice. Only by living my truth can I stay on the path.

The Six Principles of Success

> **To live a creative life, we must lose our fear of being wrong.**
>
> JOSEPH CHILTON PEARCE

To live a successful life, you have to feed your spirit and nourish your body, you have to stretch and strengthen your physical self and your mind, and you have to make regular deposits in your bank account and your relationships. When we pay attention to these six core areas of our life, success unfolds naturally as a result.

And it starts with one decision. Every day you have to consciously work on those six principles, breaking them down into actions that will contribute positively toward your long-term goals. You will need to figure out how to navigate change: how to assess the people in your life, how to find time to work out, how not to dial 1-800-TAKE-OUT when you have a craving. You need to learn how to take calculated risks and how to grow your perspective on the world.

Plotting your course through this unfamiliar territory requires a massive shift in consciousness. It takes being acutely aware of every interaction and every decision, knowing that each small step leads you toward more financial success, more career success, more relationship success, more personal success.

At first, these changes, though small, will take a tremendous amount of creative thinking to implement and effort to sustain. Over time, it will become second nature. The right decision will be already made for you and success becomes not a goal but a way of being. You won't need to weigh yourself—spiritually or physically—to see if you have reached an objective. You will own your path, instinctively attracting more positives into your life and removing that which slows your journey.

Getting Off Track

> **If you are in the way of your goals
> and dreams, I suggest you move.**
>
> ANN KAPLAN

At times, you may wake up and feel that you have done something that doesn't contribute to your journey. It may feel like your goals are too far out of reach, that bridging the divide between your current reality and the life you dream of is too difficult, impossible even. Or your eagerness to achieve might make the process feel frustratingly slow. In the beginning, we often try to cram too much into the initial steps, and then we are unrealistic about the amount of time it'll take to achieve our goals and we become disheartened.

But if we just give ourselves time, it is amazing how much we can achieve.

If you want to reach your potential, you have to be in it for the long haul. You need to stay focused on your goal and work toward it every day. And when you make mistakes, when you slip up, you pause to reflect, learn from the experience, and apply the lesson—then move forward with strengthened resolve. A detour doesn't mean you aren't headed in the right direction. It means you took a slightly longer route.

What's important, what will get us through our lowest moments, is the strength of our beliefs in both the journey and in ourselves. It's only by getting out of bed (figuratively) and facing the world, head on, with creativity and hope, by reaching for doors we didn't know existed and helping hands for guidance, that we get ahead. We need to believe in our ability to find positive outcomes:

- enough that we can get through the next minute, hour, day
- enough to keep investing in who we are
- enough to be our biggest cheerleader
- enough to have the courage to forge ahead

That belief in ourselves, which we find so attractive in other people, may be the only thing we ever truly own. So hold on to it.

Yes, you will experience moments of uncertainty. We're human, after all. It's up to you to shake off ill-feelings, embrace the journey, and work toward a life where you are at peace with your actions and decisions. Then, when the outcome isn't what you anticipated, you will be unshakable in your resolve to forge ahead, knowing you did the best you could and that more and bigger opportunities lie around the corner.

If you live your life, from this moment going forward, on the path to success, you can never really get off track.

Up Your Game

When your default position is the healthy choice, in all its renditions, the next step is to build on the positive momentum and up your game. Don't get in shape: get in great shape. Don't aim to make more money: aim to get rich. Don't pray more regularly: become a demigod! (Just kidding.)

The point is to step it up. Once you've shifted your thinking to view the world through the lens of success, broaden your focus to see the greater potential in the opportunities before you, to see solutions to everyday problems. Don't look for the cracks: see how to fix the cracks. Don't complain about the lineup: figure out how to get there faster next time... better yet, how everyone can get there faster.

Think bigger and aim higher until there are no limits in your mind of what you can achieve.

Climb Down from That High Horse

When you embrace the path to your success and let go of the self-imposed barriers in your mind, you will feel an awakening. You will feel exhilarated, encouraged, and *alive*... You will feel different than you have ever felt because you know that there is hope. When you start to understand the power you have over your existence and what your existence means, you will see how you can make change in your life and also in that of others. You will operate from a place of plenty.

And that's a profound emotion. Feeling empowered and even enlightened is what we aspire to in life. We read books to understand our existence. We grasp at life when it is threatened. And we find meaning when we let go of everything.

As you unleash the power within you, you will be keenly aware of your propensity for success, but don't let it distract you from the journey. Be grateful that you are on your path and know that you are not better or worse than someone who doesn't understand the route you're taking. Success, true success, isn't compatible with entitlement. You have not discovered anything new, though it may feel new to you—success has always been dormant within you, waiting for you to take action. Enjoy it, embrace it, but stay off the high horse of your ego.

Success Starts Now

> **There is a powerful driving force inside every human being that, once unleashed, can make any vision, dream, or desire a reality.**
>
> TONY ROBBINS

There is a reason that you reached this point in the book. You picked up a how-to because you *want to*. You want to know how to live peacefully, you want confirmation that your intuition, your gut feeling, is correct. You want to know the steps to success, to have a guidebook.

But I am telling you what you already know.

Yes, I have been abused. I have seen some of the most horrible actions that people can do to one another. I've had men try to tempt me, to buy me, to harass me. I've been cheated on. I've loaned money to "friends" only to witness their hasty exit. And I've settled for less than I know I deserve. I have made mistakes.

And, like you, I have looked for answers. I've read books. I sought higher education and studied spirituality at the feet of modern gurus. I have spent a lifetime seeking answers… only to realize that it was about the journey all along. The life I live is my success. The person I choose to be, how I make decisions, the good I put into the world—*that* is success. And it's not defined by one moment or an award; it's captured in how I live every day.

Don't like yourself? Feeling you are too far gone? Even better. Because if you can acknowledge there is something you would like to change, you're one step closer to making it happen. One step further than yesterday or one moment go.

Don't waste another minute waiting. Your success starts now. Not tomorrow, not in an hour... right now!

Today, this minute, you can choose to make positive changes in your life. Today you can focus on a new you, knowing that your efforts will not just encourage the change you seek but *be* the change. Today you can throw out excuses and doubt; you can stop looking behind and start looking ahead.

Today is the day you turn away from that which holds you back, when you shut the door to negativity and open a window to opportunity. Today is the day you say, "I can"...

... and if you don't believe it's possible just yet, today is the day you *just act like you do.*

Today is your day. And every day after it too.

EXERCISE 13: Live Success

You have the manual for success. Now put it to work!

> **The decision to make change does not happen with a sudden thought. In hindsight, you may look back and say "that was the moment" when change happened, but really it is the experiences that you have had, the life lessons you've learned, and the passing of time that brings you to the moment, to the realization that there is no better time than now.**
>
> ANN KAPLAN